CW00468995

KICKSTART YOUR ONLINE BUSINESS

CREATE AN ONLINE COURSE AND START TO MAKE SALES

SIGRUN

Difference Press

Washington, DC, USA

Copyright © Sigrun Gudjonsdottir, 2022

All rights reserved. No part of this book may be reproduced in any form without permission in writing from the author. Reviewers may quote brief passages in reviews.

Published 2022

DISCLAIMER

No part of this publication may be reproduced or transmitted in any form or by any means, mechanical or electronic, including photocopying or recording, or by any information storage and retrieval system, or transmitted by email without permission in writing from the author.

Neither the author nor the publisher assumes any responsibility for errors, omissions, or contrary interpretations of the subject matter herein. Any perceived slight of any individual or organization is purely unintentional.

Brand and product names are trademarks or registered trademarks of their respective owners.

Photo credit: Jóhann Garðar Ólafsson (Gassi)

Makeup artist: Elín Reynisdóttir

Cover design: Jennifer Stimson

ADVANCE PRAISE

"Sigrun has generated eight figures selling online courses, and in this book, she reveals the fastest path for you to make money online. Follow her straight-forward strategy to start monetizing and leveraging your valuable expertise!"

— SELENA SOO, PUBLICITY & MARKETING
EXPERT

"Sigrun. A woman in red. Like a volcano, whenever she is in action – the world is not the same like before. Her book, her method, will reshape your business, your life! Read it, you will get it – volcano power will take you and your business to the next level, no matter what."

— TANJA FRIEDEN ENERGY &
TRANSFORMATION COACH AND OLYMPIC
CHAMPION

"A must read for any online entrepreneur who wants to create and launch a successful course and grow their online business! Sigrun is an amazing entrepreneur with a simple, effective, no fluff approach that every entrepreneur could benefit from."

— MARGY FELDHUHN, CEO INTERVIEW CONNECTIONS, PODCAST HOST AND BUSINESS MENTOR

"Very often female entrepreneurs feel it's hard to build an online business. This book shows you a simple, yet well tested process to create your first online course within ten weeks, all described in a straightforward way so that it also feels doable for me and you. This book is what we need!"

— JEANET BATHOORN, BUSINESS COACH, AUTHOR, SPEAKER AND MASTERMIND EXPERT

"Anyone can study and learn information, but very few actually follow through and implement. Taking action is what creates results, and Sigrun has laid out an entire step-by-step process for how to create a successful online course – regardless of your industry or niche – for you to implement. This guide is exactly what one needs to kickstart their online business!"

— KATE ERICKSON, ENTREPRENEURS ON FIRE

"Want to start or scale your online business to seven figures? In this book, you'll learn about *Kickstart*, a unique process that has kicked off multiple million-dollar businesses. Yours could be next! This book is essential reading if you are serious about starting your online success journey."

— ELENA HERDIECKERHOFF, CEO RED DOT STAGE, TEDX SPEAKER AND BUSINESS MENTOR

"Sigrun shows in her book how she and her clients have mastered the kickstart of their sustainable and successful online businesses and how basically everyone can do it. Her framework and step by step approach reveals a simple yet fundamental plan on how to start and scale an online business. I personally love that Sigrun also addresses the various reasons (aka excuses) we might find for not starting and how we can overcome your excuses. I recommend this book to everyone who is dreaming about starting or scaling an online business and is willing to take action. This book might change your life."

— DR. JANNA SCHARFENBERG, BEST-SELLING AUTHOR, AYURVEDA EXPERT AND MEDICAL DOCTOR

"Sigrun is an extremely gifted mentor with a wealth of knowledge. I'm so glad that her wisdom has finally been captured in this book! She breaks down the path to success in a very clear, step-by-step way that anyone can follow. All you have to do is trust the process!"

— THERESA LOE, LEADERSHIP COACH

"Starting and restarting an online business takes strategy, motivation, the right support, and a lot of heart. Sigrun combines it all in her amazing book and all her work. A great way to get started or restart."

— MARIA HUSCH, HOME & SUCCESS COACH,
PODCAST HOST & BUSINESS MENTOR

CONTENTS

I dedicate this book to my parents, Guðjón Jónsson and Ásta Bjarnadóttir. I've them to thank for my belief in myself, that I can make my dreams come true, and that I can help others make their dreams come true. They are my role models in love, life, and business.

FOREWORD

You are bombarded with distractions.

Your smartphone, and laptop are likely buzzing non-stop with notifications from email, social media, and whatever chat channels you use. You've become so accustomed to the hum of these notifications that you check your phone incessantly in case there is something urgent that needs your attention.

That constant response you feel beholden to is reactive and compulsive, it's everyone else pulling you into their world and at the end of each day, you likely wonder, where did the time go? Where did my time go? What do I have to show for today?

If you're like me, you likely have big goals and dreams for the future but feel a sense of defeat when you are unable to carve out time to work on and finish what matters most to you.

You know something must change for your goals to truly have the impact you seek to make.

Jon Acuff, in his best-selling book *Finish,* says the most important day is the "day after perfect." It's the day after the day you slack off, get too busy, too distracted or fail to prioritize what you want to do. It's the day you start to beat yourself up and question whether you can really make your dreams come true.

This is the day you need a reminder that you are capable of so much more; this is when you need someone to help you kickstart that idea of yours back into action, so you don't let it die a sudden death because, for just one day, you weren't perfect.

If you've ever had a false start, an idea that didn't take off or get the traction you wanted because you got stuck somewhere along the way, intentionally or not, then this book will help you get back on track.

It's the start you need to finish.

It's more than a kickstart. It's a proven system that others have followed to get results – and if they can do it, so can you.

Set your distractions aside, put your goals back up on the board and let Sigrun guide you through what feels impossible so it becomes possible.

There is no better time to get started.

— LISA LARTER, BEST-SELLING AUTHOR OF
MASTERFUL MARKETING, BUSINESS
STRATEGIST, AND ADVISOR

INTRODUCTION

This book is based on a hugely successful online program called *Kickstart* that I created some years ago and thousands of students have completed successfully. As a direct result of the program women are starting their online businesses, taking their offline businesses online, and scaling up existing online businesses to six and seven figures. You can find out more about the program and get free resources at www.sigrun.com/kickstartbook.

In this book I will share with you many success stories from our *Kickstart* graduates and how *Kickstart* kick started their online business.

Ingrid Dach joined *Kickstart* when she was making $20,000 a year as a freelance copywriter for female online entrepreneurs, a year later, she was making $120,000 as a launch copywriter offering online courses, memberships, and group coaching programs, and two years later she was making $400,000 in her online business.

Claudia Nichterl did *Kickstart* when she was making $100,000 a year in her offline nutrition practice; a few years later, she is making close to $1M teaching integrative nutrition to health professionals through online programs.

Judith Peters participated in *Kickstart* to create her first online course, not knowing if what she wanted to teach was good enough. Several years later, she is the go-to expert for bloggers who want to use a blog to build their online business.

Those kinds of results are totally possible for anyone who is willing to put in the work and trust the process. Now for the first time ever I am revealing the whole *Kickstart* process so that you have the chance to create your own online success.

This book is for those who want to kick start their online business. It is for those who are starting from scratch in online business and those who have been in online business for a while but need a bit of a kick in the butt to take off. It is equally for those who have an online course but haven't been able to sell it successfully. It is also for those who have had an offline business and now want to take it online. More specifically, this book is for women who want to start and scale their online business. Why women you might ask? Because I am on a mission to accelerate gender equality through female entrepreneurship. I see it as my purpose to help women become financially independent; start their own business, and scale it up so that they can have a bigger impact.

Let's dive in.

HOW KICKSTART WAS BORN

OUT OF FRUSTRATION AN IDEA WAS BORN

I had been teaching online business for over four years when I started to get frustrated with my students. I had been running a twelve-month program called SOMBA (Sigrun's Online MBA) for one and half years, but something was off. I asked myself why they didn't start their online business journey despite all the great instructions I created for them. I also asked myself why they didn't finish what they started, despite me offering support through coaching calls and the community. I repeatedly asked myself why it took them so long to do the things that should take a lot less time. I realized that it was my job to find a better way to teach so that they would actually do the work – in a shorter amount of time – and *finally* have the success they deserved.

Of course, there were students who did the work and had great success. Those who actually took the time to watch my instructions and get the support they needed, saw great success in their online business. My frustration stemmed from the fact that I wanted to see more students have success. On average only ten percent of course participants finish an online course. I didn't want to accept that as a fact. I expected more of myself and my students. I wanted to see a ninety percent completion rate in my programs. I didn't know if that was possible, but I wanted to see if I could do it by changing the way I teach.

The way I taught was how I saw others teach. I had created twelve modules for a twelve-month program and my students could go through the modules at their own pace. I offered weekly support through the community. I also had monthly live masterclasses on various online business topics and monthly hot seat calls for strategic questions. I felt I offered everything my students needed to be successful in online business, but something was off, as only a handful of students were really doing the work.

It was time to shake things up and do something completely different. Summer was coming and I was concerned that another three months would pass, and my students wouldn't do much for their online business. I decided to use the summer to make them do the work that I wanted them to do in the first place. An idea was born: SOMBA Summer School! I had a rough idea of what this new online program would be about and before I knew it myself, I started to seed it. Basically, I started to say to my students, "SOMBA Summer School is coming, SOMBA Summer School is coming!" My students got excited, even those who hadn't done anything in the program over the past six months.

CREATE AN ONLINE COURSE IN THE SUMMER

I decided to make SOMBA Summer School about creating an online course. This felt like a doable and tangible project for the summer. My idea was that if my students really created an online course in the summer, they would feel inspired to continue to build their online business in the fall. I realized that some of my students were absolute beginners and didn't know how to set up an online course on an online teaching platform, so I had to make this super easy, also for those who believed they were technically challenged.

SOMBA Summer School started, and half of my students signed up to participate. This was a free program for my SOMBA students and I was quite happy that fifty percent of them decided to spend their summer going through a program where they didn't even know what would happen. They basically trusted the process – which is exactly the term we still use today in *Kickstart*: trust the process.

One hundred twenty-four new online courses were created that summer, courses that would otherwise not have been created at all. Ninety percent of those who started SOMBA Summer School finished the program. Even though I had high hopes for this summer program, I was amazed how effective the program was. The majority of the students who participated had not done anything for their online business before and suddenly they were having success and seeing the potential for more success. SOMBA Summer School (now called *Kickstart*) was exactly what I hoped for and more. It was the kick in the butt my students needed to do the work and have success.

Anke Beeren was a single mother of two teenagers and had just started her online business. Her big breakthrough came in SOMBA Summer School when she created her first online course. She became our first SOMBA Summer School winner and later our first *Kickstart* coach. Today

Anke runs a successful networking community for German-speaking female online entrepreneurs.

Gudrun Mahlberg was so fired up after SOMBA Summer School that she finally quit the job that had been draining her. With her first online course she was able to combine her childhood passion of dance and movement with her new passion of the sacred feminine. After running her course during her summer holidays, Gudrun had renewed energy and belief in herself and her business.

Hildur Jónsdóttir had overcome serious health challenges herself before she became a health coach. She was offering one-on-one counseling but looking for ways to go online with her business. She had tried to do it herself but it didn't work. It was with SOMBA Summer School that she was able to create the foundation for her first online business, and within a few years, she was running two online businesses making $1M.

Hildur Jónsdóttir's *Kickstart* experience in her own words:

"In my business, I help people with chronic health issues, chronic diseases and autoimmune problems. Having suffered severely with those myself, and with little to no help available to me, in 2015 I created my own path to recovery and put together a one-on-one program. And by 2016-2017 I was back to full health, energy and vitality after years of being really, really unwell.

People noticed how I'd managed to turn my health around. They wanted to know if I could help them too. And with demand building, I started to ask myself how can I do this? How can I scale my business?

I used to be a counselor with an office in town, but going back to in-person and having the long commute just wasn't for me any more. And so I started to think about taking it online, something I had no clue about! In January 2018 I tried to get started, but I lacked the drive to really get going. And that's when I discovered Sigrun.

I joined the very first *Kickstart* round in summer of 2018 [then called SOMBA Summer School]. Sigrun created this program for people just like me, who want to create their online course but are struggling to take action. She created *Kickstart* to get us moving, get our courses created and get ourselves out there. No questions, just actions.

When I signed up for *Kickstart*, I knew something amazing would come out of it. I just felt it was something I had to do. It is the groundwork for everything I'm doing today and in the future. Three years later, between both businesses my husband and I have, we are close to seven figures, starting from zero in 2018."

ONE-OFF PROJECT GOES INTO THE SECOND ROUND

SOMBA Summer School 2018 was supposed to be a one-off project, but the following year, I started to get emails and messages on whether I would run SOMBA Summer School again. Based on the amazing success of the first round, I knew I had to do it again, but this time, I asked my community for support, and over twenty previous SOMBA Summer School students, we call them mentors, volunteered to help me run the program.

Lena Küssner became the winner of SOMBA Summer School 2019. She is a business psychologist and brand designer. Lena was not fulfilled in her job and had therefore started to take on personal branding clients. But doing both was draining her and she needed to decide what to do next. Joining SOMBA Summer School was exactly what she needed. Creating an online course grew her self confidence and as a result she signed up new personal branding clients and made $10,000.

Merilyn Beretta had been a leadership coach for over twenty years. Despite learning from many leading entrepreneurs how to build an online business she was struggling building her own online business. She was concerned about investing in yet another program but felt this was her last and best chance. Within a year of SOMBA Summer School she crossed six figures in her online business and is now one of our coaches.

Agnieszka Gaczkowska had a passion for crocheting and was doing crocheting workshops. She had been a self-employed architect before but was now a stay-at-home mom. In SOMBA Summer School she created an online course for handmade artists and is now a coach for creators who want to teach handmade art online and those who want to sell their own handmade products over the internet.

Agnieszka Gaczkowska 's *Kickstart* experience in her own words:

"I used to work as an architect, but when I got pregnant, running around on the building site became difficult. When I had my second child I decided to slow down with my job, stay at home and be there for my kids. However, I soon started to feel a bit down. To occupy myself, I put my creativity into knitting and crocheting. I liked it so much that I organized workshops at home in which I taught my friends. Sometimes I ended up doing three workshops a week.

I didn't realize this could be a real business until I came across Sigrun. I got so hooked with the story of this lady who constantly showed up in red. She was talking about having a business that was built around your personal life, not at the cost of it. She opened my eyes to the possibility of making money doing what I love.

I come from Poland and signing up for the program was a huge investment, but I took the leap. I started living with my headphones on, soaking up everything there was to know about online business. That's when I saw the potential of what I had started. At the time, no one was offering online handmade workshops in Poland.

I created my first online course on how to crochet and it sold out completely. When I saw the money coming in, it blew my mind. I started taking my business seriously, and in addition to my crocheting online courses and offline workshops, shifted to teaching my clients how to do their own online courses and mentor them.

Financially, I can completely depend on my business. Last year I made €100,000 (which initially sounded crazy to me). My dream is to one day have a physical place where I can hold handmade workshops, masterminds and retreats.

When I came into Sigrun's orbit, I was a scared mom with low self-esteem. My only goal was to make enough money to be able to spend time with my kids. Not only did I quickly achieve that, but I started to dream big. Sigrun helped me rediscover what is inside me and gave me the tools to become a role model for my children."

After another successful round of SOMBA Summer School in 2019, it was clear I had to teach this new program standalone, and I decided to rename it to SOMBA Kickstart (SOMBA stands for Sigrun's Online MBA) so we could run it summer or winter. From September 2019, my team and I have been running Kickstart twice a year with hundreds of students each time. We continue to have a ninety percent completion rate and see our students have amazing success during and after the program. It is the program that kicks off their online business success.

Ingibjörg Reynisdóttir is a single mother who lives in the countryside of Iceland. She had recently lost a well-paying bank job when she did SOMBA Summer School in 2019. Through the program she found out what she really wanted to do and it was not what she had been doing before.

Ingibjörg Reynisdóttir's *Kickstart* experience in her own words:

"I lost my job in September 2018. I was working at a bank, and getting laid off came as a shock to me. I live in a rural area in Iceland, there aren't many high paying jobs around here, and I didn't want to move to Reykjavik. But at the same time, I realized that I wasn't made to work a regular 9 to 5 job. I'm almost 50 years old and the bank had been a secure job for me, but if I was being honest with myself, it hadn't given me what I was looking for.

I used to own a call center and make offline courses for companies on how to build up their own call centers. This wasn't the first time I got laid off, and every time I was out of work, I would restart my call center business. Once I was able to live off it for an entire year. I knew that now the time had come for me to take my business online.

I invested in a program that promised to teach me how to do that, but it didn't work for me. I didn't get a single signup for my course. At the time, I had been following Sigrun on and off for a while, and suddenly thought about her. I signed up for SOMBA in January 2019 and when I got presented with the opportunity to join SOMBA

Summer School that same year, my answer was immediately yes.

During SOMBA Summer School, I created a whole new online course for people finding themselves at a crossroads, wanting to understand where they want to go in their lives and finding the best version of themselves. I trusted the process, followed Sigrun's steps, and it turned out that I got to know myself better and found out where I wanted to go.

If online courses were cars, Sigrun's *Kickstart* is the Ferrari. I got 155 signups for my online course and made six sales, making almost $6,000 in revenue. In addition, I gave out vouchers in exchange for testimonials and ended up receiving twenty-five great testimonials, which was my main goal.

My feelings after finishing *Kickstart*? I wanted to do it again. That's why I signed up for the next program. I know that in the weeks I spent in *Kickstart* and will be spending in the next program, I will learn more than in three years of university, because I actually implement what I learn."

THE SECRET SAUCE OF KICKSTART

First of all, it is a step-by-step process. You know exactly what to do in each step and you don't need to think about anything else. We basically take overthinking out of the equation, and you just do the work.

Second, it is the detailed instructions. You know exactly how to do everything we tell you to do, and you just follow the instructions. We basically remove any tech challenges that our students think they might have.

Third, is the accountability. You know exactly when to do everything and there is a strict deadline for all assignments, so nobody falls behind. We basically remove any excuses our students might have for procrastinating.

In *Kickstart Your Online Business*, you'll learn about the *Kickstart* process itself, so you can go ahead and do *Kickstart* on your own. And if you want to get access to our detailed instructions and our unprecedented accountability, and create your online success in ten weeks, then you need to join our *Kickstart* program. You can join our *Kickstart* Insider List to be the first to know when we run the program next, and you'll also benefit from special Insider bonuses. You'll find out more about the *Kickstart* program and get access to our free resources at www.sigrun.com/kickstartbook.

Before we dive into the *Kickstart* process, let me first share the start of my online business journey with you. It is not as straightforward as you might think; I did a lot of over-thinking and procrastinating before I really started, and that's why I am so passionate about helping other women who want to build an online business and just need a bit of a kick in the butt to get going – hence the name *Kickstart*.

2

MY JOURNEY INTO ONLINE BUSINESS

MY EARLY YEARS AND MY WHY

I was brought up with the belief that I could do anything I wanted. I am very grateful that my parents instilled this belief in me. I was born and raised in Iceland and already fifty years ago it was normal for women to study and work outside the home. I didn't realize until much later that this was not normal in other modern societies.

When I was nine years old, Vigdís Finnbogadóttir became the first female president of Iceland. She was the first democratically elected female president in the world. My mother took my sister and me to her house the day after the election, and we cheered with hundreds of other people outside her home. I will never forget that day. What was special about this wasn't just the fact that she was a woman but also the fact that she was divorced and a single mother of an adopted child. She was the first single mother allowed to adopt a child in Iceland. In addition, she was a breast cancer survivor, which some of her opponents tried to use against her leading up to the elections. That's when she said her famous words: "I am not going to feed the nation; I am going to lead the nation." Vigdís Finnbogadóttir was president of Iceland for sixteen years and is considered one of the nation's best presidents. Seeing a woman, single mother, cancer survivor, and a French and Theater History graduate become a president made me believe that I could become a president too if I wanted to.

Up until I was sixteen years old, it hadn't occurred to me that other girls or women didn't believe that they can do or become anything they want.

By that time, I had been making my own clothes for several years, inspired by my mother and grandmother, and now I wanted to become even better at it by making my own sewing patterns. I joined a class to learn how to create my own sewing patterns in an eight-week course with a dressmaker. All the participants – except for me – were in their forties and fifties, so during our breaks, I wouldn't say much and just listened to the women talk about their lives. I was shocked to hear about all their unfulfilled dreams.

They had a lot of reasons why they hadn't done the things they'd dreamed of. It was because they got married, because they had children, because they had no time, no money, no skills, etcetera. I was shocked, frustrated, and angry. I wasn't angry at the women. I was angry at society.

I wasn't brought up to be a feminist, but this experience definitely made me into one. It had me asking a lot of questions.

Why can men realize their dreams? Why can women not realize their dreams? Why do women put everyone else first and themselves last? Are these just excuses or actual reasons? Or is it because society accepts these excuses from women rather than men? Is it really harder for women to realize their dreams? Could it be that women just don't believe in themselves?

For the first time, I realized that society puts bigger burdens on women than men. It's expected that women should take care of the children, their spouse, the elderly, and the home.

On the flip side, there are many women – single women, mothers, divorced mothers – who do follow their dreams. So, what's going on with the women who don't believe that they can do it? Is it because they believe their own excuses?

I made a couple of big decisions after this life changing experience.

First, I decided not to have children. I had never played with dolls or shown any interest in babysitting children like my girlfriends. I don't believe that children are the reason why women can't follow their dreams, but I didn't see myself as a mother. Even though I don't have biological children, I do have two bonus children. I became a stepmother when I met my husband and started to take care of my stepsons. They were three and four when I entered their lives, and I was able to co-parent them into two young adults who also believe that anything is possible if you are willing to do the work.

Second, I decided never to let a man stop me. Raised by parents who fell in love at the age of thirteen and are still happily married, I have always believed in love and marriage. Therefore, it was always my plan to have a loving and supporting partner at my side. At the same time, I was not going to let my partner stop me from following my dreams.

Third, I decided to always follow my dreams. I was not going to be one of those women in her forties and fifties who didn't follow her dreams. I was not going to use excuses but make my dreams a priority. I didn't want to have any regrets but be able to say at the end of my life; that I always followed my dreams.

Fourth, I decided to do my part to improve gender equality. I was furious about the inequality between men and women, especially when it comes to realizing your dreams. I didn't want to become a politician and I didn't know yet how I was going to accelerate gender equality. I was hoping that one day I would figure it out.

These four decisions have guided me throughout my life and made my life better.

I have two bonus children, which has made my life richer. I have a husband who is my biggest supporter and toughest critic, and supports all my dreams, even the crazy ones. I have always followed my dreams, even if that means moving to another country, learning a new language, starting a new study, or switching industries. Last but not least, I finally figured out a way to accelerate gender equality when I started my own business where I support women to follow their dreams, start their own online businesses and scale them up so that they can have a bigger impact too.

WHY I STARTED MY OWN BUSINESS

After being a CEO of small IT and software companies in Iceland for a few years, I found myself in Switzerland, in love but unemployed. It took me six months to find a job in a new country. The job was in a completely different field, medical technology, but I found it exciting to try something new. Fifteen months into the job, I started to experience headaches and back pain, and then came the pinching ear pain. At first, I didn't associate my pain with my job, but after a two-week summer holiday, the pain got much worse. Twenty months into the job, I had so much pain in my body that I couldn't work anymore.

I was unable to work for seven months. It was unclear what was wrong with me, although a distant friend had already diagnosed me over Skype with having Repetitive Strain Injury (RSI). RSI often comes from posture problems but also from bad working conditions. It turns out that my desk was too high and the chair too low, and on top of that, my working hours were longer than what I was used to in Iceland with almost no breaks. My doctor concluded that my job had made me sick, and I had to find another job.

I didn't have to resign, I got fired for being sick, and at the same time, I was bullied by my former employer. It was an experience I don't wish on anybody. I should have probably taken legal action, but I was too sick to do anything about it. My first priority was to heal, and finally, after five months of searching for a solution, I started to see some results. Seven months after I stopped working, I was able to start again, but this time for another company and in my home office.

I loved working from home, but I didn't love my new job. As a country manager for a new software company, I had to do a lot of cold calling, something I had never done before and didn't like at all. In addition, I had to drive long distances to potential and existing clients, and then my shoulder and neck pain would flair up. When the company went through a new investment round, I pointed out that it would be cheaper to hire someone in Germany than having someone like me in Switzerland. I was taken by the word and let go.

Within two years, I had lost my job twice and been sick for seven months. I was worried about getting sick again or never recovering fully. Therefore, I seriously started to consider starting my own business. I had always had the dream of one day having my own business. I had been running other people's businesses successfully for a decade, and it was time to start my own. I just didn't have a business idea.

At the same time, I knew what I wanted; I wanted to be location independent, so I could work whenever and wherever. I wanted to be able to take breaks in the middle of the day to go for a walk to take care of my health. I wanted to be able to spend more time in Iceland, eventually even fifty percent of my time in Iceland and fifty percent in Switzerland.

My three-month notice period was running out, and I swallowed my pride and applied for unemployment benefits. During the first interview, my contact at the unemployment office told me point blank that I was unemployable because I was overqualified and immediately suggested that I start my own business. I was shocked but positively surprised that the unemployment office would support my dream. I enrolled in a special three-week startup course and then a four-month support program for unemployed people who want to start their own business.

Overall, I spent eighteen months figuring out what I wanted to do, from the day I lost my job until I started the business I have today. I wished I had known about a book and a program like *Kickstart* when I started out. It would have saved me so much time figuring out what I should do next, what steps to take, and in which order. If you are still in the phase of not knowing what your business is about or how to really grow your online business, then you are reading the right book, and very soon, you will have the clarity you need.

MY FIRST BUSINESS IDEA

My first business idea was an online shop. I had the idea of selling Icelandic design online – home accessories and interior design items – and I thought it was a pretty cool idea. I spent time going to fairs and interviewing potential vendors and also set up a team with two women who would be my business partners. One day, I decided to see how many people google "Icelandic design." That was my reality check. It was considered a very low search term, which meant no one was looking for it, and therefore, no one wanted it.

I had a few insights that day.

First one, if you are a tourist in Iceland, you buy Icelandic design there, but when you have never been to Iceland and have no connection to Iceland, it is highly unlikely you have any desire to buy Icelandic design. You may be interested in Scandinavian design because that is what you saw in your interior magazine, but no one is going to tell you about Icelandic design.

Second, and the more important insight, if people are not looking for the solution you want to provide, then there is no point creating the solution.

I killed the online shop idea that day.

I had many other ideas in those eighteen months. I also thought of becoming an Iceland travel book author or a professional photographer or a business consultant. I looked at all these ideas in detail without actually getting started.

Each idea after the other got eliminated.

MY SECOND BUSINESS IDEA

Once a year, I travel with my family around Iceland. I have always taken a lot of pictures on our travels. I got the business idea that I could write travel books for families traveling around Iceland. I looked at other traveling books and found out which style I liked. I wanted the travel book to be short and snappy, with pictures and maps and very clear instructions on how to get to all those beautiful places and enjoy a great holiday with your family.

I wrote my first travel book and then I got stuck when it came to the maps. Google maps doesn't allow you to use a screenshot of their maps in your book. Getting permission proved to be a major hurdle. I wasn't even sure I would make any money from this book, so I decided not to go through all the hoops of getting these maps into my book. It started to dawn on me that this might not be such a good business idea. I loved traveling one week a year with my family, and I also loved creating a photo book from our travels, but turning this into a business didn't sound so appealing after all. I never finished the travel book, but I do have one photobook from all our Iceland travels.

MY THIRD BUSINESS IDEA

A decade ago, I rediscovered my passion for photography. I had been the president of my photography club in middle school and had learned how to develop my own pictures. In high school (gymnasium), I was so focused on learning that I shelved my hobby. During my university years, I started my hobby again and took a lot of pictures, and even took one photography course. I never saw it as a profession, just a passion project. Later on, I got myself a digital camera and continued taking a lot of pictures. But most of the pictures I took were just to preserve memories and not particularly good. Until a decade ago, I decided I needed a serious hobby besides my job and did another photography course. I loved it so much that I created a studio at home and got myself a professional camera and studio lights. I started to entertain the thought of whether I could do this professionally. I even had a few portrait sessions and charged for them. But then it dawned on me that I didn't want a location-based business, and I also didn't want to become a travel photographer. I just wanted to keep photography as a hobby. I mostly used the photo studio to take pictures of my stepsons, but when they became teenagers, I dismantled the photo studio and turned it into an office for my husband.

MY FOURTH BUSINESS IDEA

Before I started my own business, I was a CEO for a decade in small businesses. Sometimes I took on additional projects on the side as a business consultant. These were well-paid projects, and I enjoyed solving problems outside my day-to-day job. When I needed to make money in between jobs, it was my go-to side hustle to write business plans for startups. It was kind of cool in the beginning to get to know all these startups and go to all these meetings to get to know their ideas and plans for the future. But the actual writing part of the business plans was exhausting. I had very little information about the companies I was helping, and the founders were often not willing to spend time on their own business plans. I sometimes had to just make things up to create a good business plan. And I seriously doubt that the business plans I wrote were actually implemented. For one company, I offered to take some pictures as well because they desperately needed pictures on their website and for the business plan. The pictures were used for years but not the business plan itself. It is incredibly frustrating to be a consultant and give good advice that doesn't get implemented, so I knew in my heart that I didn't want to make this my business.

I went on a search for my true passion and the right business idea.

HOW I STARTED MY ONLINE BUSINESS

I thought I had to have a perfect website before I got started. I had no business idea yet, but I definitely needed a website, I thought. I bought a WordPress theme and switched out the theme about five times before I got so frustrated with myself. I realized that spending time on my website was not helping me make any progress. I gave myself a deadline; *two more days, and then your website is ready*, I said to myself. Two days later, I switched the website theme one more time and decided the website was ready even though I wasn't happy with it. Out of my frustration, my first blog post was born, "Why 'start before you are ready' is the only way."

My next blog posts were "How to find your passion," "Find passion through your childhood stories," and "How to find the right business idea." And more followed: "Fear is just a four-letter word." I was writing whatever came to my mind. I wasn't overthinking my themes. I wasn't wondering if someone would read my blog or not. Of course, I was hoping someone would, but it was almost like therapy for me. I was writing about things that were on my mind, things I was struggling with, and I was finding clarity as I wrote about these themes. Slowly I was getting an idea.

Around the same time, I was active in a few Facebook groups. As a former CEO and business consultant, I enjoyed answering questions in other people's Facebook groups. I had no hidden agenda, I didn't even have a business, and I had nothing to sell. At the time, I often felt I was possibly wasting my time, spending countless hours reading posts from people who were trying to build their online business and replying to them. Much later, I realized that I was unknowingly doing research while also becoming known as someone who was very helpful and knowledgeable.

By spending all this time writing blog posts and answering questions, I discovered what I was really good at and what I wanted to do. I wanted to be a business coach and help women start and scale their online businesses. I wouldn't just help them figure out how to get started, but I would also help them take their online business to six and eventually seven figures. I could have figured this out a lot faster if I had had access to a process like *Kickstart*, but instead, it took me eighteen months. It was my fifth and final business idea, and I could finally get going.

I decided the start date of my business would be January 1st, 2014. I had a website, I had written a few blog posts, and I had an email list with thirty subscribers, mostly friends and family. A month later, I had my first freebie (a free offer in exchange for an email address) and it was called "How to grow your Facebook page organically." The freebie was a success, but I quickly realized that I didn't want to be known as a Facebook expert, so I took the freebie down after only a week. Suddenly it was the middle of February, and I didn't have a freebie and didn't really have a business yet. I kept on being active in those Facebook groups, and one day, I had a wake-up call. So many were struggling with finding their passion and the right business idea. Bingo!

The idea for my first online course was born: how to find your true passion and the right business idea. Since I had a very small email list and nobody really knew who I was yet, I decided to offer the online course for free and only make it seven days long. I wanted to get going quickly to see if this online course idea was any good, so I decided to give myself a week to promote it. I had nothing ready for the course, just an idea for an outline and a fresh new Facebook group. Over 134 people signed up!

On Sunday evening, I sat down and created the first module. People loved it! And I was so inspired to see their reactions. So, the following evenings I sat down every evening and created the module for the next day. I created short videos and simple workbooks and uploaded them to the Facebook group. At the end of the seven days, I did a survey, and to my great surprise, many people had really found their true passion and the right business idea in only seven days. Some said it was too short; they would have wished for a longer time. So, I turned the seven-day course into a four-week course before I started to sell it.

I don't sell this four-week course anymore because I believe now that the best way to start is to create your first online course - hence *Kickstart* is always the first program that my clients go through on their path to a successful online business.

Still, creating that first online course was the basis of everything that came afterward. Years later, I realized that the process of how I created my first online course was when the original idea for *Kickstart* was born. Within three months of starting my online business, I figured out the best way to find out what you want to do, create a new online course and essentially kick start your online business. It took me four years until I actually started to teach this method to my students and another four years until you could read about *Kickstart* in this book.

DO YOU NEED TO BE A CERTIFIED COACH?

Who am I to help women start and scale their online business to seven figures? I didn't even ask myself that question because it was so logical to me that I could help with this. But many of the women I work with get hung up on this part. They worry about not being expert enough to teach something or not being a certified coach to be able to coach.

Let me say this once and for all; you do not need to be certified to teach others what you know or have experienced yourself. Of course, there are areas where you should be a licensed therapist or a psychologist, but in ninety-nine percent of cases, you don't need to have any special degrees or certificates to teach others.

I was a successful CEO for ten years before I started my own business. I have studied in three countries, speak three languages, and have four master's degrees. I have worked as a business consultant and I am a certified Dale Carnegie trainer. I've written business plans, and I have an MBA from a top business school. Meanwhile, I've made over $10M in my online business and helped my clients make millions of dollars. So, I have a track record and education in business, but when you call yourself a business coach, some people might ask, "Well, are you really a coach?"

Actually, none of my clients has ever asked me, but for the record, I'm not a certified ICF coach. I don't need to be because I've built a successful multiple seven-figure business myself and helped my clients build their multiple six-figure and seven-figure businesses. Before that, I ran seven and eight figure businesses successfully, doing turn-arounds, working on startups, and also completing a successful merger. Also, what I do isn't really coaching; it is teaching and mentoring.

People will want to work with you because of your personality, your skill set, your experience, and your success stories. They generally don't care what kind of degree or background you have. If you've been holding back, wondering whether you need a certificate or a degree to follow your dream, you probably don't.

There are so many things in life that we can help other people with where we don't need a degree or a certificate. Actually, my favorite photographer in Iceland never studied photography. He is self-taught, and he is one of the best photographers I know. The picture you see on the cover is from him; his name is Gassi.

The only way you're going to find out if someone is a good coach, a good photographer, or a good designer is to get to know them before you buy anything and read, watch, or listen to client success stories.

That's exactly what *Kickstart* helps you do. You will allow your potential clients to get to know you before they buy anything, and during the process, you will collect testimonials that can later be used as client success stories.

So, without further ado, let's look at the *Kickstart* process.

3

THE KICKSTART PROCESS

I n this book, I am going to share with you the best possible way I've found to create a successful online course and essentially kick start your online business. I've helped thousands of female online entrepreneurs go through this exact process in my signature program, *Kickstart*, and now I want to share this process with you.

HOW KICKSTART CAN CHANGE YOUR LIFE

Ingrid Dach joined *Kickstart* in January 2020. Within ten weeks, she created her first online course and made $8,700. Within a year of joining, she made $120,000 and in her second year of online business she made over $400,000.

Before *Kickstart*, Ingrid was a freelance copywriter selling her time. After *Kickstart*, Ingrid was an online course creator selling value instead of time. She could work less and earn more while taking care of her three children, the youngest one being only six months old at the time she did *Kickstart*.

A year after Ingrid started her online business, she was able to retire her husband so he no longer needed to work but could take care of the household and the children instead. She was also able to buy a new house with a swimming pool and a vineyard for her family and a brand-new family car.

In addition, and even more importantly, Ingrid is no longer the shy, introverted person she used to be; today, she enjoys being on camera and talking to her audience. She is a self-confident online entrepreneur who sees obstacles as opportunities and truly believes that anything is possible.

Ingrid trusted the process and followed it to the T. She didn't doubt every step of the way but instead diligently executed everything that she was told to do. She had seen the success of other students, and she was willing to trust the process to have the same success herself. And now, she is one of our greatest success stories.

Ingrid Dach's *Kickstart* experience in her own words:

"I have a PhD in physics and spent a lot of time abroad for work, but after having two kids, I decided to leave the science world. I started an online business as a copywriter and attracted a lot of female entrepreneurs, so I decided to make this my niche. I was really busy doing one-on-one work with my clients, and when my third baby was born I started going back to work after only one month.

This meant that I was spending less time with my family, and even though I worked so many hours, not a lot of money was coming in. It wasn't how I wanted to continue, and I knew something had to change.

I had been following Sigrun for a while and liked her videos and freebies, so I decided to sign up for SOMBA. I took part in the ten-week *Kickstart* sprint, created a brand new online course and made $8,700. It was a great success for me. Looking back now, it was just the start of an amazing new life and business."

After running the *Kickstart* process for five years and helping thousands of female online entrepreneurs create their first or next online course and start to make money in their online business, I am now revealing the whole *Kickstart* process in this book.

If you follow the steps in this book, then you should be able to create your online success.

If you prefer to take the fast-track and create your online success in ten weeks, then get on the Insider List for *Kickstart*. By being on the list, you'll be notified the next time we run the program, plus you'll be able to get access to some amazing Insider bonuses. This book includes the exact process that I teach in *Kickstart*. The secret to the *Kickstart* process is not the content though but the fact that our students actually take action. Therefore, your job will be to not just read this book but actually put into action the things that you read. Get on the Insider list and get access to our free resources at www.sigrun.com/kickstart book.

WHAT IS THE KICKSTART PROCESS?

It is a step-by-step process to help you create your first or next online course and start to make sales in ten weeks. Below you are going to learn more about the details so you know what is coming.

• **Step 1 – Meet your dream client:** The most important foundation of any business is a clear ideal client. If you

don't know who your ideal client is, then you don't know
where and how to market your business, and it will be very
difficult to make sales. That's why we start with your ideal
client, and you're going to figure out who it is even if you
haven't made any sales yet.

• **Step 2 – Find out what they want**: Once you know who
your ideal client is, you can talk to your ideal client. You
can survey your ideal client, and you can interview them.
Basically, you are going to talk to real people and find out
what they really want. This is the only way to create a
successful online course and business – you figure out
what they want and give it to them.

• **Step 3 – Design the course your ideal client wants**:
Once you know what your ideal client really wants, you
are going to come up with a course idea that solves their
biggest problem. It is going to be exactly what they want.
You are going to map out a four-week course with four
modules, so it is an easy yes for your ideal client to sign up
and participate.

• **Step 4 – Promote the course before you create it**: Once
you've designed your course (but not created it yet!), you
can start to promote it. You are going to offer it for free for
the first time because you need feedback and testimonials
– and it builds your email list with future buyers. You want
to get as many signups as possible so that your email list
grows and you get more testimonials, plus have more
potential clients.

• **Step 5 – Create the course while you run it:** You are
going to create the course with your ideal clients, so it
becomes exactly what they want and need. Every week you

are going to ask for feedback from your participants and adapt your course to their feedback. That's why you don't want to create the course upfront but only create one module at a time. This is how we ensure that your online course is sellable in the future.

• **Step 6 – Get feedback and testimonials from your course participants:** Throughout the course, you'll be asking for feedback so you can adapt your course to the needs and wishes of your ideal client. In your final feedback form, you will also be asking for a testimonial. Sharing testimonials is one of the best ways to sell your online course in the future.

• **Step 7 – Design your next program:** The magic of offering a free four-week course means that by the end of the course, there will be participants who want to continue the journey with you. This is your chance to make sales and help those who want to learn more from you and make an even deeper transformation. This next program needs to be the natural next step after the four-week course.

• **Step 8 – Celebrate and sell your next program:** After the four-week course is finished, you invite your participants to a celebration call. During the celebration call, you celebrate the transformation that your participants have gone through with them, you teach them a final lesson that ties into your offer – and finally, you present your offer – and start to make sales.

WHY A FOUR-WEEK ONLINE COURSE IS BEST AS A FIRST COURSE

Four weeks is the minimum length for an online course. Anything shorter is typically not called an online course, but a "challenge" or a "boot camp" or maybe a "mini-course" but is not considered a real online course.

Four weeks is twenty-eight days, and that's just enough time to make a transformation. Anything shorter is just not enough time to make a lasting change.

Four weeks is not too long when you want to try out a new idea. After four weeks, you know if you want to do this again or maybe do something else.

Four weeks is also the perfect time for someone new to get to know you, like you and trust you enough to eventually buy from you.

WHY YOUR FIRST OR NEXT ONLINE COURSE IS GOING TO BE FREE

The biggest challenge most aspiring online entrepreneurs have is a lack of an audience. They have very small or non-existent email lists and not a big social media following. Offering a paid program when your audience size is small leads to disappointing results of no or very few sales. So, the first thing you need to do is to increase your audience size and grow your email list.

Typically, you offer a freebie in exchange for an email; basically, you create a free gift in the form of a checklist or an eBook, and when someone wants to download your free gift, you get their email onto your email list.

Offering a free four-week course is the ultimate freebie and way more attractive than the typical freebies out there. I once read that your freebie should be so good that people want to pay for it. That's exactly what you are going to do. Your free course is going to feel like it is worth $500, and therefore, way more people are going to sign up for it than if you had a regular freebie. That's exactly what you need and want to grow your email list with future buyers.

WHO CAN CREATE AN ONLINE COURSE?

Many think that online courses are only for business coaches or marketers. That couldn't be further from the truth; actually, most of our *Kickstart* students are neither business coaches nor marketers. To inspire you, I have pulled together a list of all the different types of coaches, consultants, teachers, trainers, and overall service-based entrepreneurs who have created an online course with the *Kickstart* process.

- All kinds of singers
- Vocal coaches
- Interior designers and architects
- Clothing and color stylists
- Sewing teachers
- Dog trainers and veterinarians
- Positive psychology coaches
- Mindset trainers
- Transformational coaches
- Relationship and dating therapists
- Photographers and graphic designers
- Visual artists of all kinds
- Math and science teachers
- Branding experts and strategists
- Social media managers
- Language teachers
- Sales trainers

- Health coaches
- Nutritionists
- Fitness trainers
- Doctors and medical practitioners
- Lawyers and accountants
- Copywriters and bloggers
- Event planners
- Astrologists
- Dance therapists
- Financial advisors
- Podcasters
- Virtual assistants
- Energy healers
- Intuition coaches
- Professional organizers
- Farmers
- Shamans
- Wellness coaches
- Confidence trainers
- Chinese medicine practitioners
- Productivity coaches
- Midlife coaches
- Web developers
- Yoga teachers
- Futurists
- And so many more...

Hilkea Knies is a singing teacher and trains vocal coaches with her own method. She hadn't considered creating an online course because she thought it wouldn't work with singing. But then the pandemic hit and she had to take her teaching online. Then the idea of an online course started to sound right and she joined *Kickstart*.

Hilkea did so well that she became the winner of our January 2022 cohort.

Hilkea Knies' *Kickstart* experience in her own words:

"Actually, I hadn't really thought about an online business until Covid-19 came along, because something like that seemed difficult with singing.

I love music but I was never much into technical things. So when all of a sudden everything went online, I was lost at first. All these new terms, all these things that needed to be understood, I was totally overwhelmed.

I run an institute with a colleague and we started to work more and more online. There were the two of us so we could divide the work. That was good, because I slowly lost my fear of the technical challenges and could see in the one and a half years that it was also wonderful to work online with singing.

I listened to Sigrun's courses, which she offered as a "freebie", in addition to my work at the institute. And then in the winter of 2021 at her 12 days of Masterclasses it was already clear: 2022 I will finally get in.

And for me it was a complete success. I was able to master the technology, all the things I didn't like; like making ads, designing surveys, interviewing people, it all started to be really fun for me.

And I became quite successful. In the beginning, I didn't really know if 200 people in the Facebook group was good for my four-week free online course. Whether 32 people were good in my upsell course. But I was very happy and my students left awesome testimonials for me.

There was also something else that attracted me to *Kickstart* from the beginning. The question of why we women are not more successful and Sigrun's desire to support women in particular. I was able to take my money mindset to a new level with Sigrun's help and when I even became the Kickstart winner at the end, I couldn't believe my luck.

Kickstart fully deserves its name, because it was the start of a whole new professional perspective and allowed me to take my dream job as a singing teacher even further into the world."

Kasia Krasucka calls herself a motivational language teacher, teaching Danish to Polish people living in Denmark. She didn't know what an email list was when she started to create her first online course with *Kickstart*. Her lack of knowledge about online terms didn't stop her from achieving six figures in her online business in less than a year.

Kasia Krasucka's *Kickstart* experience in her own words:

"I joined *Kickstart* without having an email list. Actually, I didn't even know what an email list was. I had a dream of having an online business in order to experience a location independent freedom. Within a year of *Kickstart* (and a lot of committed and consistent work) I ended up with $100,000 in revenue and an email list of over 700 people!

In my online business, I decided to focus on one of my expertise, namely language teaching. I became a creator of online Danish courses for Polish speakers. *Kickstart* became also my way of healing after a toxic relationship. It was a great way of distracting my thoughts from personal life and putting all my energy and determination into creating my first online course."

WHAT EXCUSES DO YOU NEED TO GET RID OFF?

There are many excuses that pop up and stop you from even starting.

I'm going to list a few here and if any of those apply to you, just know that you are not alone. Now it is time to let those excuses not stand in the way of achieving your dreams. Instead of using excuses you can use them as reasons why you should follow your dreams.

• Wrong Age

> Too young or too old? The concept of age is irrelevant when it comes to *Kickstart*. We have women who are 70 years old and creating their first online course, and we have women who are in their early 20s creating their online businesses. You are never too young and you are never too old to make your dreams come true.

• No Support

> I will not deny that it is hard to start a business when you have no support from family or friends. I am not talking about financial support although that helps of course, what I am really talking about is emotional support. If you don't have any support from home then it is really important to find that support through a community of like minded people. Those communities exist and one option is to join the *Kickstart* program where so many women have found friends for life.

• No Time

> You probably know what I am going to say here. We
> all have 24 hours in the day and we have a choice on
> how we spend those hours. If something is a
> priority for you, you will find the time. All kinds of
> women, who felt they had little or no time, have
> gone through the *Kickstart* process; single mothers,
> mothers with young children, pregnant mothers,
> women with a full time job, women taking care of
> sick parents, women on holiday, women moving
> from one country to another, women going through
> a divorce etcetera. Despite their challenges and
> commitments these women made *Kickstart* a
> priority - and so can you.

• No Money

> The same goes for money as for time. When some-
> thing is a priority for us, we'll find the money for it.
> Investing in yourself is the best investment you can
> make. If making this investment is too much for you
> right now, then start by reading this book, that
> doesn't cost you anything. Once you are ready to
> implement what you read in this book, then it is
> likely you need to get support. I want to make one
> thing clear though, I never suggest anyone goes into
> debt when starting their own business. Find other
> ways to fund your business start.

• No Skills

> Many women think they are not good at technol-
> ogy. This is a myth we need to bust once and for all.

Women are good at anything they put their mind to. If you decide to learn tech, you can learn it. It is more a question of your mindset than your ability. This book doesn't include technical instructions so you can read it without thinking about the technology. When you are ready to implement *Kickstart* and join our *Kickstart* program then you'll find detailed technical videos for every step of the *Kickstart* process.

• Perfectionism

This one is so common that I think literally every woman is a perfectionist. The key to combat perfectionism is to have deadlines that force you to take action in a limited amount of time. This has several benefits; you learn to make fast decisions, you learn to use the 80/20 rule and most of all, you get used to the saying "better done than perfect". The *Kickstart* program is ten weeks for this very reason so when you read the book you need to set your own deadlines to get rid of your perfectionism - or you join the *Kickstart* program and my team and I will help you overcome this excuse in no time.

Claudia Silberborth hadn't started her online business and still had a full-time job when she joined *Kickstart*. She was so proud to start to make sales that she is now working part-time so she can work more on her online business. Her perfectionism was standing in her way in the beginning but with *Kickstart* she overcame it.

Claudia Silberborth's *Kickstart* experience in her own words:

"My biggest challenge was to actually decide to create my four-week online course without any preparation in advance. I am a perfectionist and I would never have promoted a course that just existed in my mind and was not already finished. But it was fun to create the content on the go. I overcame my fear of not being perfect!"

Jaconette Mirck also struggled with perfectionism. She would probably never have put out her course materials if she didn't have the short time frame and deadlines in *Kickstart*. As a result she has reduced her need for making everything perfect.

Jaconette Mirck's *Kickstart* experience in her own words:

"My biggest challenge was feeling that the materials weren't ready to be shown to the public. Kickstart helped me to use the "better done than perfect" approach. Even though I wasn't satisfied with some of the materials, I shared them with my participants, and they loved them. As a result of the *Kickstart* process, I got rid of some of my perfectionism."

Nadine Härtinger didn't just suffer from perfectionism but she also had very limited time due to her very young child. Still, she didn't use that as an excuse to go through *Kickstart* but made her online course and online business a priority.

AND THEY FINISHED ANYWAY...

Our *Kickstart* students have experienced all kinds of challenges and still finished the process.

• Therese Blom was highly pregnant when she joined *Kickstart*. She expected her baby to arrive after the ten-week program, but her baby had different ideas. The baby arrived just as she was running her online course. But Therese didn't let that stop her, and she finished the program on time and made $20,000!

• Ingrid Dach had a six-month-old baby when she joined *Kickstart*, and she had two other young children. She made arrangements with her husband and used the nap times to work on her business and the *Kickstart* process. She saw her children as a reason to keep on going – and she finished with $8,700 in sales!

• Andrea Oberdorfer's computer got hacked in the middle of the *Kickstart* process, and she lost all her files. She didn't let that stop her and borrowed an old computer from her parents to continue running her online course. Her positive attitude and resilience were an inspiration to other students.

These are just a few examples of the challenges our students have experienced during the *Kickstart* process - and they still finished and so can you.

Now let's dive into the process of creating an online course that sells starting with your dream client.

4

MEET YOUR DREAM CLIENT

WHY MOST ONLINE COURSES DON'T SELL

The reason why most online courses don't sell is that nobody wanted them in the first place. There was only one person who wanted this online course, and that was you!

You may have an idea for an online course, but in order to create an online course that sells, you first need to find out what your ideal client really wants. They may or may not want your online course, and you don't want to find that out after you've created it.

Many women come to me when they have already created an online course; some have even spent weeks and months creating it. But then they try to sell the course and just get crickets – because nobody asked for it!

Mia Brummer had created nine online courses before she joined *Kickstart*. Nobody had asked her for those online courses, and she hadn't asked her clients what they wanted. Mia had been a therapist for twenty years, and when the pandemic hit, she knew she had to take her business online and become a coach. She had been trying to create online courses and sell them, but it wasn't working for her. It was an epiphany for her to ask people what they want. It was like everything she had been trying to do before fell into place like a puzzle, and she was able to generate $55,000 within ten weeks of joining *Kickstart*.

Mia Brummer's *Kickstart* experience in her own words:

"I started as an entrepreneur in 1989. My field was personal and professional development; until 2004 I mainly worked one-on-one. In 2004 I started my seminars in personal development in and with nature on a small scale. With my seminars, I accompanied people on a two-year journey of development. Pretty quickly I expanded my offer on request and offered counselor training. My offers were only advertised by word of mouth. For 15 years I had a five-figure annual revenue and was happy with it. I was a one-woman show and had a work-life balance.

At the end of 2018, I felt a shift. I became dissatisfied with my business orientation and looked for a new challenge. My participants felt the change and sales plummeted. In 2019 I found out about an international certification program in online business and applied for it. Together with 100 people from all over the world I went through a tough boot camp for ten weeks and learned how to design online courses and acquired valuable social media skills. What I didn't learn was how to sell.

As I continued to produce one online course after another, I only sold them to my small circle of fans. In my opinion, I really tried everything to make adjustments. I changed the course content, did courses in English, German and Spanish, produced podcasts, posted daily, and didn't understand why I wasn't making more sales. I was completely burned out, frustrated, and questioning my expertise.

During the pandemic, I worked almost around the clock and produced more content than ever before. But the lack of a sales strategy caused my sales to stagnate.

In 2021 I had 39 offers, a podcast, a YouTube channel, and a blog... and my revenue had slipped into the mid-five-digit range. A burnout raged in me but I didn't want to give up.

In December 2021 I read about Sigrun's offer to plan for 2022 and I signed up. The five days with Sigrun were an absolute eye-opener for me. Tough and crystal clear, I realized that I had left the executive chair in my company to be a content creator. For me it was clear after the five days; a turnaround had to take place and the best coach for this big project was Sigrun. I signed up for Sigrun's Momentum without hesitation.

The biggest toad I had to swallow at the beginning was the task of concentrating on ONE offer. For two weeks I couldn't sleep, tried to wriggle myself out of it, haggled, tried to let at least two or maybe even four of my offers survive. In the end, I gave up. I devoted myself to the *Kickstart* process and learned an important mantra that still supports me to this day: trust the process.

I started with a blank sheet of paper and completely reconsidered my knowledge, my skills, and my expertise. The beginning was ONE idea - which was based on my many years of experience but took a completely new direction. And: it was not just a head birth, but was put through its paces under Sigrun's watchful eyes. Directly with the ideal client.

Kickstart was an exciting journey. To create in a community, to have buddies facing the same challenges, to be motivated, to be picked up, to receive feedback, and to learn valuable skills that you learn to implement immediately - for me there is no better way to learn.

I lived for these ten *Kickstart* weeks, I breathed *Kickstart*, I produced for *Kickstart*, I dreamt of *Kickstart*, I was *Kickstart* - and it paid off. In the end, I made 55,000 with the sale of the follow-up offer. I am completely convinced of the *Kickstart* process and can only say that if you are really serious about getting started online, then invest in it."

HOW TO CREATE AN ONLINE COURSE THAT SELLS

You ask your ideal client what they want, then you create an online course for them, and then they will buy it.

Before you can ask your ideal client what they want, you first need to get clear on who your ideal client is.

Every successful business I know has one ideal client in the beginning. They don't have many ideal clients – just one. As businesses grow, they may or may not have more ideal clients, but their success is based on that first ideal client.

So, who is your ideal client?

If you are just starting out, you make the person up.

If you have been in business for a while, then you pick a real person or a combination of a few real people and merge them into your ideal client.

Close your eyes and visualize this ideal client in front of you.

• Is it a man or a woman or someone who doesn't specify as either?

• What's their age? Are they married or single?

• Do they have children, and if yes, how many and how old are they?

• Do they live in the city or out in the country?

• What kind of car do they drive? Or do they prefer not to have a car?

• Do they live in a single home, an apartment, or something else?

• Are they employed, or are they an entrepreneur?

• What kind of education do they have?

• What's their profession? What do they do for a living?

• What is their income per year?

All of these questions are called demographic questions. They give you an idea of who your ideal client is, but they don't help you know if your ideal client has the problem you want to solve.

Besides starting to know who your ideal client is, you need to know what the problem is that you want to solve.

BIG PROBLEM VS. A SMALL PROBLEM

A successful business has one ideal client and solves one problem. I bet you can solve many problems, but in order to be successful online, you can only solve one problem at a time.

In order to build a sustainable business, you need to break up the one problem you want to solve into what I call a big problem and many small problems.

An example of a big problem is a "healthy lifestyle."

When you think of a healthy lifestyle, you probably get many different ideas and not necessarily the same ideas as me, and that's okay. Therefore, it is important to get much clearer on what you mean by a healthy lifestyle or what I call breaking it up into smaller (and more digestible) problems.

An example of a small problem is "losing weight."

When you think of losing weight, you are getting much clearer on what the problem is, and it is not as fussy as a "healthy lifestyle."

When you create an online course, you are tackling one of the smaller problems and not the big problem. Why? Because the big problem cannot be solved in an online course as it is at least a six-month, year-long, or even a multi-year process.

I help high-achieving self-doubting women start and scale their service-based online business to seven figures. That's my big problem that I want to help female online entrepreneurs solve. This cannot be taught in one online course. It is a three to four-year process, so I have to start with a "smaller" problem like *how to create an online course that sells.*

So, how do you find out what your first small problem should be?

In the beginning, you make a guess, and then you find out what your ideal client really wants, but first, we need to get a lot clearer on who this ideal client is.

It is not enough to know it is a woman, thirty-four years old with two children, married and living in the city with a $30,000 annual income as an employee.

You need to know what is called psychographics.

• What keeps her up at night? What is she worried about?

• What books or blogs does she read to get more information?

• What T.V. shows or videos does she watch to find out more?

• Who does she follow online to get inspiration and information?

Then you need to dive deeper and get clear on how she feels about the small problem you want to solve. Let's call the small problem you would like to solve X.

• What comes to her mind when she thinks of X?

• What is her biggest challenge when it comes to X?

• What has she tried before when it comes to X, and why didn't it work?

• What's the ideal outcome when it comes to X?

• What does she think could be her obstacles on the way to solve X?

A lot of people will read this chapter and move on to the next one without actually taking the time to write down the answers to these questions. This is a mistake.

The ideal client exercise is the most important exercise

you will do for your business. Without an ideal client, there is no successful and sustainable business.

You have to know who you are selling to in order to sell anything.

You have to know who should buy your online course before you create it.

I know it is a bit annoying to read a book and have to do an exercise; I am definitely guilty of just skipping the exercises because I want to move onto the next chapter. And for the rest of the book, you are welcome to do that. If you just do one exercise within this book, then do the ideal client exercise. You can thank me later.

Under the link www.sigrun.com/kickstartbook you can download an ideal client workbook that I have created for you. In this workbook I have more detailed instructions and questions for you on how to get super clear on your ideal client. Under the same link you'll also find other great resources related to the *Kickstart* process.

To give you an idea of how an ideal client sounds, here are two examples for you from our Branding Guide created by merging our most successful clients into two characters.

MEET IDEAL CLIENT EXAMPLE ONE

Forty-six-year-old Dr. Johanna Bauer is a certified nutritionist and traditional Chinese medicine practitioner (TCM) with a passion for plant-based medicine. She's an expert in her field and has published over a dozen recipe books on topics like herbal tinctures, plant-based meals, and immune-boosting nutrition. Although she's passionate about these topics, her books bring in little revenue. She loves seeing lives transformed by wholesome food, which spurred her to open a cooking studio nearly a decade ago. There, she's hosted events and cooking classes for her community with the help of a part-time assistant. She's a natural educator, and people are inspired by the way she makes complex health and nutrition ideas simple and fun. On the outside, her business looks successful. But the expenses of her studio absorb most of her revenue. The stress of her situation has worn heavily on her body, mind, and marriage. Recently, she suffered an injury that made her in-person live cooking classes impossible to teach. Between this injury, a global pandemic that caused the world to transition online, and a personal crisis, Johanna was desperate to make a change in her business. She sold her studio and immediately felt relieved from the burden of those expenses. She currently offers one-on-one virtual nutrition and TCM services to long-standing clients but knows that this isn't sustainable. She's now in a position where she's ready to restructure her business to more successfully and efficiently share her knowledge with the world and build real wealth for herself.

MEET IDEAL CLIENT EXAMPLE TWO

Olexa Černý, PhD is a thirty-eight-year-old mother of three based in the Czech Republic. Smart and ambitious, Olexa earned her PhD in physics and spent her late twenties traveling the world, attending academic conferences, and collaborating on research projects in pursuit of a tenure track position. By the time she had two kids, she realized that this was neither sustainable nor was it what she wanted to do long-term. With a natural knack for writing and strategy, she shifted to copywriting – a job that she can do from home while she raises and homeschools her three young children. She works mainly with female entrepreneurs and loves the connections that she makes. However, all this one-on-one work leaves her drained and emotionally tapped out. Her business doesn't give her the financial flexibility to save a lot of money for a long-term break, so she went back to work within a month of giving birth to her third child. She works long hours and makes lackluster money, which makes it hard to justify spending so little time with her children and husband. Despite having a PhD in physics, building a business from the ground up, and being a terrific mother to three young children (one of whom has special needs), she lacks confidence. She knows that her business could be different but doesn't know how to make it happen. She loves to learn from business experts online and absorbs as much knowledge as she can through social media and free resources. However, she suspects that she needs mentorship and hands-on support in order to make a big shift.

Once you've defined your ideal client, you need to verify that your ideal client actually exists and find out what this person really wants.

5

FIND OUT WHAT THEY WANT

TALK TO REAL PEOPLE

In order to find out what people want, you need to talk to them. It sounds like common sense, but most people don't do this. Instead, they go ahead and create whatever they want to create, only to be disappointed later when nobody buys what they've created.

I'm going to make sure this doesn't happen to you, and that's why I will share with you exactly what you need to do to make sure that people want what you will create and that you are able to sell your online course.

After you've defined your ideal client, you need to verify that your ideal client actually exists and find out what they really want. You don't find this out by asking directly, "what do you want?" You need to become like a detective and figure this out without asking them directly what they want. Since I am a fan of detective stories, I actually love this part of the process.

For this to work, you need to summarize your ideal client description into one sentence.

Example: My ideal client is a female online entrepreneur who is working one-on-one and trading time for money. Her challenge is lack of time and being paid too little for her expertise. This ideal client wants the opposite of her struggles: to earn more money and be valued for her expertise. She would love to have more freedom, spend more time on her hobbies and/or with her family, and see her business grow and have more impact.

Then you turn your one-paragraph ideal client description into a survey introduction.

Example: *I'm looking for female online entrepreneurs who want to stop trading time for money and instead have a scalable online business where they can work less and earn more so that they can enjoy more freedom while at the same time have more impact. Is that you? If so, then please fill out this survey. By filling out this survey before DATE, you have a chance of winning a one-hour coaching session with me.*

Who am I? I'm one of the leading business coaches in Europe and a multiple seven-figure entrepreneur. I help female entrepreneurs start and scale their online business to seven figures and beyond. I have worked with over 5,000 clients, and over 100,000 have attended my free trainings.

With the one-paragraph ideal client description and the introduction, you are ready to create a survey for your ideal client. Your survey should be short, no more than ten questions, and mostly open-ended questions as you want to get their words and their descriptions.

Download a sample survey at www.sigrun.com/kickstartbook

Once you've set up the survey, you start to promote the survey on social media and to your email list if you have an email list. You only want your ideal client to fill out this survey, no one else, and therefore, you can include one question in your survey to double check that the right people are filling out the survey; otherwise, the results will not be reliable.

Katja Brunkhorst has had a website branding and copy business for a few years with her husband. She was clear on who her ideal client was in the website business, but when it came to starting an online coaching business, she struggled for a while to define her new ideal client. She kept on making compromises and trying to make the two ideal clients be the same person, but after a while, she had to realize that her online coaching client was a totally different ideal client. That's when her online coaching business started to take off.

Katja Brunkhorst's *Kickstart* experience in her own words:

"I was a scholar of literature and worked in advertising agencies before I had an online business, but I've always been too much of a free spirit to be able to stand the politics and hierarchies in those fields. That's why I jumped into self-employment as a copywriter in 2015. I founded my own business and my husband joined me in creating websites and branding. After a while, I was even able to retire him from his art director job.

But while we loved working one-on-one with our high-end clients, something was missing. We soon realized that we could only take on so much more one-on-one work between us, but still wanted to grow our business. We knew we had to start focusing on list building and really leveraging our expertise through online courses and group programs.

I had joined SOMBA (Sigrun's Online MBA) for the first time in 2017 and was intrigued by the idea of building my own tribe and teaching online. *Kickstart* didn't exist back then. Few years later I returned to join *Kickstart*.

I had heard so many great things about this program and knew it was right for me - a highly sensitive, at times overthinking perfectionist like myself.

What I got out of *Kickstart* is priceless. I confirmed who my ideal client is and got incredible feedback from participants of my course. My upsell conversion rate was over 20% and I ended up making almost $10'000 - all during a beginning recession!"

Make sure you don't compromise your ideal client. It is one person with a well-defined problem that you want to solve - and not someone with many different unrelated problems.

Your goal should be to get a minimum of ten survey responses but ideally 100 so that the responses help you to find out what your ideal client really wants.

Once you've got enough responses, you are going to pick three people who filled out your survey and sound like your ideal client and ask them if they are willing to be interviewed. The reason we interview three people is that it is not enough to interview one person, but once we interview five or more people, we actually start to get the same answers again and again; therefore, three people is just perfect.

You should conduct the interviews over a video conference software and record the interviews so you can transcribe them later. The questions you ask in the interview are not so different from the questions you asked in your survey, but now you have a chance to go deeper and ask even more questions. Remember to ask open-ended questions and let your interviewee speak without interruption; be careful not to make any assumptions or put words in their mouth. The goal of the interviews is not just to verify that your ideal client actually exists but also to get the words that your ideal client uses about their problem and their ideal solution. That's why you are going to transcribe the interviews afterward so that you have all the words that your ideal client uses in one place. This helps you speak to and attract your ideal clients in the future.

HOW TO FIND A GREAT COURSE IDEA

There is a process to finding great course ideas. To create a course that sells with ease, you want to fulfill three criteria.

The first criterion is about finding out what your ideal client really wants and needs right now and something that they are willing to pay for. There are things that we want, but we don't necessarily need, and there are also things that we want and need but are not ready to pay for.

The second criterion that needs to be in place is your ideal client's awareness of the problem. It is not enough that they are aware of the problem; it also needs to be something that they are actively looking for a solution to, directly or indirectly. We call this having a high awareness of the problem.

The third criterion that makes your course stand out and become highly attractive, meaning you can charge higher prices for it in the future, is its uniqueness. There are a gazillion courses out there. If your course is exactly like someone else's course, it will be harder to distinguish between the two or more courses, and you don't want your ideal client constantly wondering which course they should buy. The first time you create your course, your first online course, you shouldn't worry too much or even think much about this part, but once you start to market and sell your online course, you need to pay special attention to this: making your course unique.

With those three criteria in mind, you now put your detective hat on and go through your survey responses.

If you have less than 100 responses, you can read each response, but if you have hundreds or even thousands of responses, you can take a sample of 100 and look closer at them. You are still welcome to take a bigger sample once you have recognised a trend in the answers.

First, look at three questions in particular: the question where you ask them about their challenges, the question where you ask them about their ideal solution, and the question what they worry about at night. Scan one question at a time and look for patterns. I highly recommend having your answers in a spreadsheet so you can highlight anything that stands out to you. Pick a color that highlights similar answers. You don't need to read each response carefully for the first scan. Once you see a pattern, then you take the time to read the response in detail so you can really understand what the real problem is.

Your interviewees also give you good ideas; take a look at the transcriptions of the interviews to verify what you are finding out in the surveys. Do you see a recurring theme? What are the majority of survey respondents and interviewees saying? Overall, you don't need the interviews to determine your online course; the purpose of the interviews is a different one. The interviews are for you to be able to use the words that your ideal client uses.

EXAMPLE OF GREAT COURSE IDEAS

• Write your book in thirty days: It is very specific and timely and solves a clear problem. It feels possible, with the right structure and support, to write a book in thirty days.

• Find the right business idea: It is again very specific and feels doable in four weeks. It is a crystal-clear promise of what the outcome is.

• Four steps to a healthy breakfast: It is very clear what will happen in the program, and it will attract participants who want to learn how to have a healthy breakfast and will not attract those who are not interested.

EXAMPLE OF NOT SO GOOD COURSE IDEAS

• Build your online business in twenty-eight days: It is too broad and doesn't solve a clear problem. Building an online business takes time; it can take one year to achieve six figures and three to four years to reach seven figures. There is no way you can teach everything about online business in only four weeks.

• How to live a healthy life: It is way too broad and doesn't solve a specific problem. It may attract all kinds of people with all kinds of problems, and there are also no specific outcomes, so you don't know if the goal of the program has been achieved or not. That can lead to a lot of unhappy participants.

• Lose 10kg in four weeks: This is a specific but unrealistic promise. People will not believe that it is possible to lose 10kg in four weeks and will therefore not sign up, and those who sign up will be unhappy as they cannot achieve the goal. In addition, this kind of promise will lead to issues on social media as social media platforms ban you from promising something that cannot be achieved.

Jane Von Klee saw herself as a copywriter when she joined the *Kickstart* process and therefore wanted to create a course in copywriting. But by doing the surveys and interviews she realized that her audience actually wanted something different from her. So she niched down and created a course on search engine optimization (SEO). Today she is one of the go-to SEO experts in Germany.

Jane Von Klee's *Kickstart* experience in her own words:

"I started out as a copywriter in 2019 and did *Kickstart* for the first time in the summer of that year, thinking I would create a course in copywriting. However, when I surveyed my audience, I found that they were much more interested in learning about SEO, so I did a course about that and people loved it.

I still do copywriting, but my focus shifted to SEO. I help female entrepreneurs to appear on page one in the Google search results so they can attract more clients to their website.

After my first *Kickstart* round, I joined Momentum to continue working with Sigrun. Half a year later, I was able to quit my part-time job and fully commit to my online business. However, I was always a bit worried about not earning enough money.

I signed up for another round of *Kickstart* because I wanted to create a second course combining SEO and copywriting. *Kickstart* was perfect for this – I already knew the process and had my target group.

More than 200 people signed up for my course, I received love letters and wonderful testimonials, and my participants even started to promote my course to friends and colleagues while it was still running. When I did my upsell, I had a conversion rate of the percent and made $25,000.

Something changed in my mind. Even though I had been successful before, I still had this fear of not making enough money. But now, I started thinking: If I can do it once, I can do it again. I have something people want, and they like me as a person and the way I teach. I feel much more secure and confident now.

What I like about working with Sigrun is that she's very straightforward and doesn't accept excuses. Sometimes I really needed this, especially when I was scared, or hesitant. During the upsell process, my first group was full after only 24 hours. I thought about closing the doors, but Sigrun told me to sell as many spots as I could. I kept the doors open and in the end, sold 21 spots. I don't think this would have happened without Sigrun. I appreciate how much energy she has, and that she believes that everyone of her clients can achieve their goals."

Lorena Hoormann didn't have any idea for an online course before she joined *Kickstart*. During the designing and promotion phase she also changed her online course idea a few times. Most *Kickstart* students use only online tools to promote their online course but Lorena took the unusual approach of creating flyers to attract her dream client and was able to ask people directly why they were not signing up for her online course. That's when she realized that she had to adjust her topic to give her audience what they really wanted.

Lorena Hoormann's *Kickstart* experience in her own words:

"I didn't have any idea for a course before joining. And even during *Kickstart* I changed quite often. Not only during the design phase, but also during the promotion. I remember I printed flyers with my title and subtitle and the target group. I went through two districts in Vienna, Austria to spread those flyers at houses and my boyfriend helped me. One day later I thought: Sh*t, the clients I thought about while designing the course, the ones I talked to in the interviews, and those who filled out my survey, they are not signing up! And then I asked them and got the feedback that my course, especially directed at leaders, didn't attract the people I wanted because they didn't see themselves as leaders. So I switched the course topic and made it a lot more down to earth. And this was just the right decision. These people are on my email list until now and are buying from me.

During the *Kickstart* process I really started to see myself as an entrepreneur and got the courage to go out with what I am doing as an expert. And this feels just so good."

Veronika Matysová already had a ten week online course on how to write a fiction book when she joined *Kickstart*. She thought of not joining since she had already sold it before and she didn't see why she should learn how to create an online course that sells since she had one already. She also didn't have an idea for a four-week online course but then an idea started to form and she decided to join. Her idea for a four-week course was a course on how to prepare for writing a fiction book, including the outline and the book cover, which turned out to be the perfect path to her ten-week course.

Veronika Matysová's *Kickstart* experience in her own words:

"I joined Sigrun's free training for the first time in summer 2021. I had started an online business the year before and during that summer I was about to quit my diplomatic posting in Paris (working for Czech Ministry of Foreign Affairs) and move back to Prague, to freedom.

In my online business I teach how to write a book, focusing on "fiction" books. I have already written eight fiction books myself. I knew that I would be able to make a living from being a book coach. I was prepared to live a modest, but free life in my small but nice apartment at the outskirts of Prague, helping people make their dreams about writing a book come true. What I didn't know was how big a change Sigrun would bring to my life and that this dream would be just the beginning.

Before joining *Kickstart* I had two launches of my book writing online course, each time making about $4,000. With *Kickstart* I made $14,000 and two months later launched again and made $10,000. The next launch after that was again almost $11,000.

Also before Sigrun I didn't have a "signature course" and a follow up course. I had random courses, which I liked and people did too, but there was no sense of a path. Sigrun taught me that I should have a main course that I will keep repeating and gradually scale, and a follow up course for people who will want to continue with me.

One thing that surprised me about *Kickstart* was to be confronted with my scarcity thinking. I wasn't aware of it at all, I had never heard about the scarcity mindset versus abundance mindset before I joined *Kickstart*. When Sigrun did the exercise with us about moving from one to the other, it opened a whole new world for me. Each time I

felt something "wasn't possible" or "didn't work", I learned
to approach it "how can I make it possible" and "how can I
make it work". I am an encyclopedic example of a person
with a scarcity mindset turned into a person with an
abundance mindset. Thanks to it, I believe that anything is
possible in my life (just as it is in everybody's life)."

Once you have your online course idea, you need to
design the course itself. You are not creating the course
yet, just designing it.

6

DESIGN THE COURSE YOUR
IDEAL CLIENT WANTS

Your online course should be four weeks with four modules where you release one module a week. We call this a drip-fed course. The advantage of a drip-fed course is that everyone is doing the same thing at the same time, and participants are more likely to finish the modules on time. On the other hand, all-access courses allow participants to go faster through the course but also have the downside that many participants feel over-whelmed when they get access to all the content at once and never finish the course.

You are creating a course that will transform the participants' lives in some way, whether it is personally or professionally. That means you need to create assignments in your course that the participants need to do in order to have that transformation. Nobody's life or business is transformed by just watching videos. Participants have to take action; they have to do something. That means giving them weekly assignments, one to five assignments per week, depending on the intensity of each assignment. It is easier to get participants to do something small than something big; therefore, your goal should be to break assignments down into achievable steps because it is better to create several assignments than one big one.

The first time you run your online course, I recommend you just record one video per module. The next time you run it, you are going to have to re-record all the modules, and then you should break each module up into three to five lessons, where each lesson is one video. The way I think about modules is that one module contains what I can expect my students to complete in a week. A lesson is one task so if you have multiple tasks then break them up into multiple lessons.

In more detail, you take your solution and break it down into four parts that make sense for each module, and then you break each module down into three to five assignments that participants are supposed to complete each week. The assignments are automatically the lessons in the module. If there isn't a clear assignment, then it probably isn't worth creating a lesson for it.

EXAMPLE COURSE OUTLINE

In 2014 I came up with my first online course, a four-week course called Passion-A-Thon. The name combined passion and marathon and the idea was to shorten a process that takes way too long, hence the marathon name. Too many aspiring entrepreneurs wonder months and even years what their real passion and the right business idea is. This course shortened the process dramatically and within four weeks you had the answer to your question.

The course outline for the Passion-A-Thon course went like this:

- Welcome

  ○ Introduction

- Module 1

  ○ Assess Your Current Life
  ○ Rediscover Your Childhood Passions
  ○ Survey Your Friends and Family
  ○ Create Your Vision

- Module 2

  ○ Create Your Dream Lifestyle
  ○ List All the Things You Like Doing
  ○ Must-Haves vs. Nice-to-Haves
  ○ Brainstorm Your Passions
  ○ Brainstorm Business Ideas and Revenue Models

- Module 3

  ○ Your Ideal Client
  ○ Assess Cost and Time
  ○ Business Ideas Matrix
  ○ Describe Your Ideas and Business

- Module 4

  ○ Your Why
  ○ Pitch Your Idea
  ○ Reflect
  ○ Next Steps

You are going to promote a free four-week online course. Even though it is free, you need to get super clear on who you want to participate, what they will get out of participating in the course, and you need to give future participants some details on how the online course works – and also why it is for free this one time only.

COURSE NAME

The name of your course needs to be short (one to six words), and ideally, it describes what the course is about without going into too much detail. *Kickstart* is, for example, a good short name for an online program. It gives a hint of what the course is about, but you still need a big promise to explain what the course is about.

Good course names are:

• Kickstart

• Momentum

• Passion-A-Thon

• Sales Every Day

• Launch & Sell

BIG PROMISE

The big promise tells the ideal client what kind of results they can expect from the program. Don't be too vague here, be clear and be a bit bold in your big promise. Even if you know that not everyone can achieve the big promise, your job is to think about your best students and what they can achieve – that's your big promise! Make the big promise eight to ten words at most.

Examples:

• Find your true passion and the right business idea

• Write your book in thirty days

• Make social media work for you

WHO THIS COURSE IS FOR

Your online course is for your ideal client, but now you are going to describe your ideal client in a way that your ideal client feels spoken to vs. writing about your ideal client, so it serves you. Make this fifty words or less, so it is super clear who you want in your new online course.

Example: *This course is ideal for female online entrepreneurs who want to sell value instead of time, are moving from one-on-one coaching to online courses, or just starting out in an online business. This is equally applicable for first-time course creators and those who are creating their second or third online course.*

COURSE BENEFITS, FEATURES, AND DESCRIPTION

In the course description, you want to focus on the benefits of each module and less on the features, although you should mention some features too. Keep your course description 100 words or less.

Benefits Examples

• You will learn how to come up with a course idea that sells

• You'll create a course outline for your new online course

• You'll know exactly how to promote your course, so you get the most amount of signups

Features Examples

• The course is four weeks and has four modules

• You'll get access to one module a week

• There is a weekly coaching call on Thursdays at 10am CET

• All coaching calls are recorded, and you get access to the replays

Course Description Example

Step-by-step instructions on how to create an online course that your ideal clients actually want. You'll learn how to figure out what your ideal clients want help with and how to create a great name for an online course. You'll learn how to promote your online course to your ideal client. You'll learn how to run and create the course at the same time while also getting feedback from participants. After the course is over, you'll learn how to get testimonials. Then in the final step, you'll learn how to do an upsell to your course participants.

Once you have the name of your course, the big promise, who it is for, and what the course is about, then you can start to promote your course.

Barbora Mikulášková joined *Kickstart* in June 2021. She didn't even know she was supposed to create an online course in the program. Barbora had been making and selling her own handbags and was thinking of starting to sell sewing patterns to grow her business. Instead of being disappointed that *Kickstart* was not a program to teach her how to sell her sewing patterns online, she dove right into the program and created her first online course. A year later she had built an online business selling sewing courses making over $170,000.

Barbora Mikulášková's *Kickstart* experience in her own words:

"Before *Kickstart* I was building my own brand with hand-made bags. I learned how to sew and make patterns by myself and I fell in love with handbag sewing. But as the brand got bigger, I lost the joy of sewing, because I spent most of my time on admin work. I also missed having a community and people around me to talk about my passion. So when my second daughter was born I knew I needed to change something.

At first I thought about selling sewing patterns but I knew I didn't want to build a second business on my own, I wanted a shortcut in terms of professional support. So I was listening to podcasts, where I heard about Sigrun's free training. That was my chance.

Sigrun was great and I felt I needed her support. But I had no money to buy the *Kickstart* program. So I put on a special handbag sale. If my clients wanted to support my journey, they could buy a discounted handbag. I was really emotional, how many wanted to support me. Thanks to the huge support, I earned just enough money so I could invest in *Kickstart*! My baby was four months old when I jumped in.

Since I was so busy making the money to afford *Kickstart*, I didn't really read the sales page so I had no idea we would be creating an online course! I was thinking I would build my business by selling sewing patterns... Well, no regrets at all!

Before *Kickstart* I was making $8,000 a year selling handbags.

With *Kickstart* I made $21,000 and thanks to this I was able to join Sigrun's Momentum. In my next launch, via Sigrun's Launch & Sell program, I made another $21,000 with my signature program. My clients wanted to continue so I sold them another program, and made another $16,000. Unbelievable.

In April 2022, ten months after I joined *Kickstart*, I had a one million Czech crowns launch (OMG, still super unbelievable) and I crossed $100,000 in revenue since *Kickstart*.

Now, not even a year after the first sale in *Kickstart* I have made $170,000.

I started with zero people everywhere. Now I have 7,700 people on my email list, 4,800 in my Facebook group, over 500 in my paid programs and thousands in my free programs. In one year. That's a lot of handbags....

To sum it all up, I absolutely love online business! It's genius! It works exactly as Sigrun teaches us. My job is pure happiness for me, and so is my life as well. My biggest breakthrough is that I can make my own life as I envision it. I can do whatever I want to, I can have more time and money, I can spend more time with my kids and husband doing a job which is really helpful to others. Unbelievable. I am living my deepest dreams now."

In the next chapter, you'll learn how to promote your online course.

7

PROMOTE THE COURSE BEFORE YOU CREATE IT

Once you have the signup page for your online course ready, it is time to promote your course. Give yourself at least ten to fourteen days to promote your free, four-week online course. More time doesn't necessarily mean better results.

There are dozens of ways to promote your course, but the most common ways are your email list if you have one, and social media. By the way, you don't need a big social media following to promote your new online course, and you also don't need to go ahead and create new social media pages; you can just use your personal profiles wherever you already have a profile. If you have no social media profiles, you will have to rely on other ways to promote.

In order to promote your course, you need to create promotional posts and/or emails. Over a ten to fourteen-day period, you are going to create many social media posts and emails, so the following example is just one way to promote your online course.

Example of a promotional post: *Still trading time for money in your coaching business? Learn how to have more clients and make more money without spending more time in your business. By creating an online course, you can serve more people at the same time and have a bigger impact. Join this free training to start creating your first online course.*

Remember to always add a good picture or video to your posts. Text alone is not enough to catch people's attention; therefore, you always need a good visual too.

Once you have a visual and a good copy for promoting your online course, you need to promote it in as many places as possible.

Go to our *Kickstart* resource page and download a checklist of all the places and ways you can promote your online course - www.sigrun.com/kickstartbook

BEST WAY TO PROMOTE YOUR ONLINE COURSE

The key is to promote on the channels that you are already active on and where it is most likely that your ideal clients hang out. If you've never been active on Twitter, there is no point creating a Twitter account and starting to promote on Twitter. If you are active on Facebook, then you go and promote on Facebook. If you don't have a Facebook page, then just stick to your personal profile; you can always create a page later. Stick mostly to two channels that you like and are most likely to give you access to your ideal client.

Promoting an online course is a marathon and not a sprint. Typically, people tend to promote a lot in the beginning and then promote less and less. You need to continuously promote your online course throughout the promotion period of ten to fourteen days. Even if you don't see many signups come in, you don't give up, and you continuously look for ways to promote your online course. You might be surprised how many people sign up at the last minute.

One of the biggest mistakes I see in the promotional phase is to aim too low. Many of those who go through the *Kickstart* process think – before they learn otherwise – that having a small group is better, so many of them aim for only ten to twenty participants. The opposite is true; your goal is to have as many signups as possible. You are creating a scalable online course, and the number of participants in your free online course will determine the next steps in your online business. By having more participants, 100 or more, you have more options to grow your online business.

Anna Rischke was in one of our first *Kickstart* rounds. Initially, she didn't go all in with her promotion; she was limiting herself. Her idea was to have only twenty participants – she didn't want to have more. Somehow she thought it would be more comfortable to have a smaller intimate group in her first online course. It was only through the encouragement of our *Kickstart* coaches that she realized that she needed a lot more than twenty people to build an online business. Anna changed her approach and decided to go all in on promoting her new online course. Every day she stepped more out of her comfort zone and told people about her online course. In the end, she was able to have sixty-eight participants, and this was the kick she needed to start her online business. Anna created two online courses with *Kickstart* which are still her main programs today.

Lee Chalmer's biggest insight in *Kickstart* was noticing that she would normally hold herself back but because of the process, she kept on going. I asked her to get as many signups for her course as possible, and when Lee reached 150 signups after only the first thirty-six hours, she thought about stopping. But through encouragement from our coaches and mentors she kept going and ended up getting 720 signups! This was a really important life lesson for Lee, to allow herself to stretch and see what is possible.

There are some expected and unexpected benefits from promoting your free online course. Through your promotion more people will get to know you and what you do, we call this brand building. Some of these people will not be interested in your free online course but they might want to interview you or have you speak at their event or they want to buy something else from you right away.

Ragnhildur Vigfúsdóttir's biggest breakthrough in *Kickstart* was the huge exposure it created for her and her programs. She got several new opportunities thanks to *Kickstart*. A woman approached her when she was showering before a swim and introduced herself. She had attended her free online course and asked her to give a workshop at her company. This is the only time I've heard someone negotiate a price nude!

Ragnhildur Vigfúsdóttir's *Kickstart* experience in her own words:

"I started my own business in 2015. I was a certified coach with a diploma in positive psychology and had a couple of other certifications (Strength Profiler, Dare to Lead, team coach etcetera). I worked mainly with individuals and companies. Running workshops and lecturing about communications and mindsets. I came across Sigrun on Facebook and attended one of her free workshops. She got on my nerves and as a certified Nero-Linguistic

Programming (NLP) master coach I knew I should look inside myself!

I realized that even though I was urging people to step into their courage I did not step into mine. I was stuck in the "never - ready - trap". I was always preparing, getting new certifications but having problems with my PR and pricing. I joined Sigrun's Launch & Sell program and then *Kickstart* (should have done it the other way around) - and went from having no email list to having 800 people on my email list. I had 300 signups for my free online course and sold nine spots to my next program. Sigrun's formula just works.

Now I have created three new courses and ran them - offered one of my courses after *Kickstart* and ran it and created a group that is still meeting and learning together.

Kickstart made me take steps and actions I would otherwise never have done. I gained more confidence in the technical stuff that had stressed me before and drained me. I got people on my email list that have bought other programs from me. Now more people know about me and what I have to offer. I love sharing what I know and doing it in a creative way.

I loved the process; not too much information - more doing than thinking :) I felt like somebody held my hand and urged me to take baby steps. Stop preparing - start doing. You are ready."

Anything is possible for you, too – if you trust the process. Next up is creating the course while you run it.

8

CREATE THE COURSE WHILE YOU RUN IT

WHY YOU SHOULD SCRUM YOUR COURSE

You are going to create your course while you run it.

The advantage of creating your course with your participants is that you end up with a course that is exactly what your participants want and helps them get results.

If you create your course before it starts, you are building it on the assumption that you know best what your ideal clients want, need, and what will help them the most. You don't!

Only the participants of your online course really know what they want once they are in your online course, so creating your course upfront is a complete waste of your time.

I had to learn it the hard way that people don't know what they want until they actually see it.

I used to run a website agency. It was my first CEO job back in 2004. Our ideal client was one of the top 100 companies in Iceland, universities, and media outlets. When the University of Reykjavik reached out to us and asked us to design their new website, we were ecstatic – it was our perfect ideal client. The project started with a requirement meeting like any other project. The university held multiple internal meetings and took their time in creating what we thought was one of the best requirement documents we had ever received. With a detailed description, my team got to work on designing a website that exactly matched those requirements.

The design went through a rigorous approval process and finally got approved. And then, my team of programmers created the actual website. We were so proud of our work and were excited to present the new website to the team at University of Reykjavik. Only to find out that this was not exactly what they wanted… You can just imagine our surprise. It was all according to their requirements, and they had approved the designs.

Why didn't they like the website when they finally saw it? Because people don't know what they want until they actually see it. This episode with the University of Reykjavik led me to implement a new method into our website design process. Instead of doing massive requirement documents upfront, we allowed our clients to introduce new requirements along the way. Basically, we created something and got their approval before we went to the next step. This is what most modern software companies do today, and the method is called SCRUM (short for Systematic Customer Resolution Unraveling Meeting).

I asked myself, *why don't we use SCRUM for online courses?*

After helping thousands of course creators, I can assure you that SCRUMming your online course is way better than the traditional method. Your success is practically guaranteed.

CREATE THE FIRST MODULE

While you are promoting your free four-week online course, you start to create the first module of your course. And you are not going to create modules two through four yet!

The only thing that needs to be ready when your participants start your online course is the first module. Don't create the lessons, videos, or anything for the other modules yet.

You'll release the first module on a Monday, and then later that same week, ideally on Thursday; you send out your first feedback survey. In the survey, you ask for feedback on the first module and the expectations your participants have on the next module. Your participants have only a few days to send in their answers. You have them ready on Sunday morning when you create the next module. At the end of each week, ideally on Thursday, you also offer a Q&A call (a Questions and Answers call) so participants can ask you questions. You'll also learn a lot from their questions in how you need to structure the rest of the online course.

The following weeks run exactly the same way, with a new module every Monday, a Q&A call on Thursday, and another feedback survey. In the last week, week four, you add some additional questions to your feedback survey that ensures that you can collect testimonials. One of the reasons you are running this course for free is to get those testimonials.

While you are running your online course you are also connecting with your participants. Use the time to get to know them, their wishes, their needs and wants. What are they struggling with the most, what can you do differently next time to make it easier for them. Start to take notes that help you improve your online course in the future.

It may sound scary to create your online course while you run it, but all our *Kickstart* students can attest that this process works and is way better than creating a course upfront - only to find out that your students don't like it, or you can't sell it.

Judith Peters loved the clear structure in *Kickstart* and especially the part on creating an online course. Despite being a university lecturer and having eight years of copywriting experience she wasn't sure that her online course would be good enough. Contrary to her doubts, her first online course was a huge success, and since then she has created multiple online courses that all turned out to be great too. By creating online courses and getting feedback she realized she could niche down to her passion, blogging. Today she runs a blogging academy and teaches women how to use a blog to build an online business.

Judith Peters' *Kickstart* experience in her own words:

"Three children, a freelance business, no time for myself, huge ambitions but a lot of questions and little perspective: That was my situation in December 2017, at the end of my third maternity leave. I was the breadwinner of the family and besides being a freelance copywriter since 2009 I was also a lecturer for copywriting at a university. I charged way too low prices and needless to say: I was completely overworked.

Approaching my forties, I felt that I had no future in advertising agencies. So, I knew I wanted to start something new - but what? Then I stumbled upon this woman in red on Facebook. And somehow I just knew that this woman in red, Sigrun, was the perfect person to work with. Back then, I had no idea about online business. Okay, I had a website, but my blog had been dormant for some years, and my newsletter... Well, let's better not talk about it. I'd been working for a lot of digital agencies, but I didn't even see the possibility of starting an online business myself! I mean, what should I teach people? I didn't see that my huge knowledge and experience as a copywriter, a creative, and a blogger was of worth, if not as a freelancer!

So, in January 2018 I decided to jump into this adventure with Sigrun, not even knowing what exactly was awaiting me. Because I didn't have a clue what I could teach and sell people. I just knew: This is going to be an adventure, and it will give me a perspective. Back then, I had forty-seven newsletter subscribers. Now, over four years later: When I write a newsletter to my thousands of subscribers, more than forty-seven people unsubscribe – and I love it: More unsubscribes than I had subscribers at the beginning of my online business to start with! Back then my income oscillated between zero (due to maternity leave) and €60,000 (my best year as a freelancer, that was 2015 between two maternity leaves). Now I make multiple six figures, have bought a house, and rented out our old apartment. My husband and I couldn't be happier working together in our family business.

When it came to creating an online course, I really appreciated the clear structure in *Kickstart*. I always knew exactly what to do and when. From the outside, creating and launching an online course might seem so easy. But there's so much to it: creating content, setting up tech, making videos, adding subtitles, setting up landing pages, writing sales emails, reaching out to potential participants,

cheerleading in the course group, and so on. These activi-
ties need to be coordinated, otherwise, you'll lose yourself
in a thousand tasks. That's why following the *Kickstart*
process is so valuable - you never lose yourself."

In the next chapter, I'll teach you what questions to ask
in the weekly feedback forms.

9

GET FEEDBACK AND TESTIMONIALS FROM YOUR COURSE PARTICIPANTS

The key to getting even more interest and sales is having someone say that what you are selling yields success. Testimonials from real people are worth gold. That's why you are running your online course for free – to get testimonials. Once you have testimonials, you can start to sell your online course.

At the end of your online course, you are going to ask for testimonials. But even during the four-week online course, you can ask for testimonials every single week, based on what has already happened. This gives you a clear indication of how people are receiving your course.

At the end of each week during your four-week course, you send out a feedback survey. It is best to email out the survey and use a survey software to capture the answers. The first three weeks the survey is the same, but at the end of the fourth week, your survey is a bit different, as you want to get a final testimonial that you can use for the sales page of your online course.

Here are the questions to ask each week:

• What were your three biggest takeaways from this week's module?

• What questions came up for you that you would love to get answers to?

• In the next module we'll do (fill in the blank). What would you love to see me cover about that topic?

•Anything else you want to add?

In the final feedback form you add a couple of questions that serve as a testimonial:

• What are your three biggest takeaways from the course overall?

• *Testimonial*: A friend asks you about the course because they are interested in participating. Describe what you liked and what you got out of it. Please be as specific as possible.

See a sample survey by going to www.sigrun.com/kick startbook.

Save your testimonials in a good place; you will not use them right away, but you will when you sell your four-week course in the future. To make sure your testimonials have the biggest possible impact, make sure to ask for permission to use the testimonials with the corresponding person's name and picture. To get the most value from your testimonials, you can interview those who were your best success stories and left the best testimonials for you.

Iris Seng was one of our first *Kickstart* students and she is still selling the online courses she created back then. She loved receiving feedback every week from her students, it gave her the boost she needed to continue, ideas for the next modules, and she started to collect testimonials which have helped her sell her online courses again and again. Iris used *Kickstart* to create a side business as she didn't want to quit her full-time job yet as an architect. When Covid-19 hit and the architecture company needed to restructure, Iris took her chance and left the company to focus hundred percent on her business. She just turned sixty and is now a business story architect.

With feedback from the first three weeks in your hand, your next step is to design a program to sell your participants.

10

DESIGN YOUR NEXT PROGRAM

The magic of offering a free four-week online course is that some of your participants will want to continue working with you.

So, the question you should ask yourself at the end of week three of your online course – not earlier! – is, what is the next natural step for your participants?

Again, you are going to play detective and read between the lines of your weekly feedback responses and figure out what your ideal client would love to learn next. You can also use posts and comments from your community to get ideas of what they want next.

Claudia Nichterl has a PhD in nutrition and had written twenty books when she joined *Kickstart*. She was a true expert in her field but was overworked, and undervalued her own expertise. She already had a twelve-week online course outlined but she had never sold it and didn't know how to sell it. Using a free four-week course to attract her dream clients was a game changer for her.

Claudia Nichterl's *Kickstart* experience in her own words:

"I was stuck making €100,000 in revenue for nine years. When I started working with Sigrun, I learned how to take my business online, increase my prices, and multiply my revenue without exhausting myself. From a solopreneur with a part-time assistant, I went on to build a company with eight employees, and just achieved my first seven-figure year.

I'm a nutritionist and expert in traditional Chinese medicine (TCM). I wrote over twenty books, was running my own cooking studio with cooking classes, and helped my clients to eat healthy.

My business was generating good revenue, but my expenses were very high. For nine years, I was running a six-figure business, but I had no growth and no profit. I was consistently making €100,000 in revenue, but I had €90,000 in expenses.

2017 was my most challenging year. I injured my shoulder, got divorced after twenty years of marriage, and was exhausted from my work. I had so many expenses that there was barely anything left for me. That's when I knew I needed to change the way I was running my business.

In 2018, I started working with Sigrun. She took me by the hand and gave me step-by-step advice on how to create my first ever online course. Having her online community around me, receiving constant support really helped me.

I ended up selling my signature course to eighty participants and loved it – I could work at my pace, reach people even outside of Vienna, Austria and make a big impact with little effort. And the best thing: by selling my online course to more people I was able to generate the same revenue as before, but without exhausting myself.

I finally had time to look after myself, and I felt that now, I could truly help people eat better and live healthier.

Over the next two years, I got clear on my vision and came out of my comfort zone. I opened the doors to my own academy for integrative nutrition and created a new signature program.

Sigrun helped me understand that with my expertise, I could change my audience from individuals to professionals and increase my prices in the process. Before, my highest priced program was €420. Now, I'm selling an eight-month program for €5400. I'm finally getting paid for my value and experience, while my participants receive good value and can immediately implement what they learn.

In 2019, I went from €100,000 to €200,000 in yearly revenue, and in 2020 I reached €500,000. And in 2021 I achieved €1M. My goal is to educate 1,000 health professionals. If my 1,000 students work with another 1,000 people in the next few years, we will make at least one million people healthier.

From a solopreneur with a part-time assistant, I went on to build a small company with eight employees achieving seven figures in revenue. I always dreamt of achieving this, but I didn't know how, and I used to believe I couldn't make it happen. Now, I know it's possible, and that I can do more. I know this business will help me achieve my mission. I'm clear and focused, and Sigrun helped me with that. Being able to make an impact in the world gives me so much energy, and I'm incredibly grateful for it."

Claudia created her first four-week online course with *Kickstart*. Her free course was called "Power Breakfast" and the big promise was: "Find your individual power breakfast." She had over 900 signups for her free course which completely took her by surprise. After the free course she was able to sell eighty spots to another online course. Her next online course was called "Simple Eating Easier Living" and was twelve weeks.

DESIGNING YOUR UPSELL

We call the next program "an upsell" because you are selling your participants something more expensive than what they bought before. They got your four-week online course for free so anything you sell afterwards is automatically an upsell. A downsell would be something that is less expensive than what you sold before.

When you design your upsell you need to read carefully through all the feedback forms for hints of what they would like to learn from you next. You'll also look out for any suggestions your participants make in your community. At the same time you are also the expert and you know what your participants need next. Remember, you can only sell people what they want to buy so your participants need to be aware of what would be the best next step. You can create this awareness in a celebration call which we will explain in the next chapter. First, your job is to design the upsell.

Elisabeth Engel joined SOMBA (Sigrun's Online MBA) in 2017 and participated in the first *Kickstart* round in 2018 when it was still called SOMBA Summer School. Back then she focused on the topic "limiting beliefs" but over the years she was searching for a better niche. She knew by participating in *Kickstart* again, she would find it.

And she did, by listening to the participants of her new four-week online course.

Elisabeth Engel's *Kickstart* experience in her own words:

"Kickstart has impacted my business in a very big way and in a way that is bigger than numbers. The huge impact of *Kickstart* for me is to have really found the niche I want to work with for the next few years and I have been looking for since three years. As a result of *Kickstart*, I am redesigning my signature program (my upsell) right now, that is running for the 3rd time and adding 3 new modules about visibility and high-end marketing. For the very first time I am teaching marketing (and I learned from the best, including Sigrun) in a group program and not only with my one-on-one clients.

My biggest challenge really was to do the surveys every week for all the modules. I had some limiting beliefs coming up for myself; I didn't want to bother them too much while they were doing all the homework, and steal their time. I got over my limiting beliefs, and that's how I was able to make €20,000 with my upsell.

Kickstart is an amazing process that I love so much and have done already three times, each time creating a completely new successful online course."

EXAMPLES OF A FREE 4 WEEK COURSE VS. UPSELL

• Example 1:

  ○ 4-week course: Find your business idea
  ○ Upsell: Start your business

• Example 2:

  ○ 4-week course: Create your tagline
  ○ Upsell: Learn to market your business

• Example 3:

  ○ 4-week course: Map out your signature talk
  ○ Upsell: Create your signature talk

In your upsell, you can offer a one-on-one coaching package, a group program, an online course, or a membership. It depends on how many signups you had for your free four-week course on what is the best option.

• Example of a one-on-one package: six weekly sessions over six weeks, each session is forty-five to sixty minutes, email support can be included, there is no community support. In a one-on-one package you don't need to create any content upfront since the program is tailored for each participant.

• Example of a group program: three-month group program with six participants, weekly modules, weekly sixty-minute sessions where everyone can speak up, no email support, a community with all participants.

• Example of an online course: eight-week online course, weekly modules, weekly Q&A call where people can submit their questions, no email support, a community with all participants.

• Example of a membership: annual or monthly payments, no end date, monthly fresh content, weekly Q&A call where participants can submit questions, a community with all participants.

What type of program you should pick depends on how many signed up for your free four-week online course.

If you have less than 200 signups, then a one-on-one package is the best option. If you have more than 200 signups but less than 500, then a group program is the best option. If you have more than 500 signups but less than 2,000, then an online course is the best option. And if you have more than 2,000 signups, you can consider a membership, although an online course is also a great option.

Some people get stuck on what to offer as an upsell because they overthink or overanalyze all the possible options. Remember that the upsell is the next natural step for your ideal client. If you have some non-ideal clients in your free four-week course, you need to resist the temptation to create something that will suit them too. Stick to your ideal client and create the best next step for them.

One crucial mistake to avoid is to offer an upsell that sounds too similar to your free four-week course. People do not want to buy something that they already got for free. So even if you feel that your participants would appreciate more time and need to go deeper into the same topic as your free four-week course, do not try to sell them something that they already feel they got for free. Your next natural step is a new program.

SEEDING YOUR UPSELL

Seeding means that you can talk about something coming but not what it is. Don't try to sell your next program or even tell people that there is a program. Just make people curious about what is next and why they need to show up for the celebration call.

Seeding means that you are not selling your upsell yet, but if you know what you are going to sell *and* you are getting questions about what happens next, you can mention that you'll cover it in your celebration call. This will make your participants more excited about joining the call.

In the next chapter, we dive into what a celebration call is and how to use the call to present your offer and start to make sales.

11

CELEBRATE AND SELL YOUR NEXT PROGRAM

I n the last week of your free four-week online course, you announce a celebration call. This celebration call should ideally be in the following week after the course finishes, as you want to give your participants time to complete the course first.

CELEBRATION CALL

The celebration call is a way to celebrate what your participants have achieved in the last four weeks. You basically want to remind them of the transformation that they have gone through. This is also an opportunity for you to make an offer, tell them about the next step in their journey, and invite them to sign up for this next step.

Here is the outline of what you do in the celebration call:

• Celebrate the transformation your participants achieved

  ○ Share success stories and testimonials

    ○ Allow participants to share live on the call

• Teaching part where you show what comes next

    ○ Teach something related to the next step in their
    journey (this allows you to talk easily about your
    next program)

• Make an offer with your next program

    ○ Talk about the benefits of your next program
    ○ Invite them to join the program

• Offer a Q&A

    ○ Answer any questions that come up
    ○ Tell them how they can take the next step

Example of what you could teach:

- How to have sales every day in your online
  business
- How to scale your online business to $20K
  months
- How to successfully launch your signature
  course

The teaching part of your celebration call should not be longer than thirty minutes.

You will announce your upsell during the celebration call – and not before!

That is the start of your open cart period, and you will close the cart six days later.

Your attendees need to have filled out their final survey

and testimonial beforehand, and therefore, the deadline to fill out the final feedback form is on Tuesday, the day before the celebration call, assuming your celebration call is on Wednesday.

To incentivize your participants to show up for the celebration call, you will tell your participants what is going to happen on the call:

- You are going to teach something that you have not covered in your four week online course
- You are going to have participants share best practices from the course
- You are going to tell them what the next steps are
- You are going to give out prizes
- You are going to celebrate!

START TO MAKE SALES

You make an offer for your upsell in the celebration call. Depending on the price of your program, you will offer them to purchase right away, or you will offer a discovery call. If your program is less than $1,000, then you can offer them to buy right away; if your program is more than $1,000, then you offer them to book a discovery call.

If you are still wondering whether you should offer a one-on-one coaching package, group program, online course, or a membership, it's a number's game.

On average, only three percent of those who sign up for your free four-week course will buy your upsell. This number could be lower or higher, but when you prepare your upsell, you need to calculate with three percent so you create the right program for your participants.

If you have 100 signups, three might buy. That's why

offering a one-on-one coaching package is the best option for anyone with less than 200 signups.

If you have 200 signups, six might buy. A group program has a minimum of six participants. That's why you need to have 200 or more signups to offer a group program.

If you have 500 signups, fifteen might buy. That's why you could offer an online course if you have 500 or more signups, but a group program will also be a good choice.

If you have 2,000 signups, sixty might buy. That's why you could offer a membership if you have more than 2,000 signups, but an online course will also be a good choice.

What you want to avoid with your upsell is offering a program that has too few participants therefore, offering a one-on-one coaching package will be the best option for most people going through this process for the first time.

HOW TO MAKE AN OFFER

During the celebration call, you will make an offer. Before you make an offer, you want to talk about what are the best next steps for your participants after the four-week online course is finished. Then there will be a natural transition to talk about your offer. To make sure you don't forget anything, it is best to use slides and show step by step why your offer is the answer.

Here is the outline on how to present your offer:

- Transition from your teaching part
- Introducing your online program
- Big promise
- Benefits
- Features

- Modules (only to be included if you are not offering one-on-one coaching)
- Bonuses
- Investment
- How to join (apply first or directly sign up)
- Deadline to sign up (or apply)
- Q&A

It makes sense to have a Fast-Action Bonus (FAB) so that your participants take fast action. A fast action bonus expires in twenty-four hours or less. All other bonuses can be included all the time.

Make it easy for people to buy from you by having a very clear sign-up process. Take payments through popular payment processors so that you don't have to write an invoice.

FORTUNE IS IN THE FOLLOW UP

When you make an offer you need to follow up. Some may buy right away but others need more time and a lot of reminders. It's your job to follow up and remind people when your offer expires. I recommend making your offer available for six days which means if you do your celebration call on a Wednesday, your offer expires the following Tuesday.

Daily reminders are needed throughout the open cart period. You can automate the reminders, but it also makes sense to do personal outreach to those who show the biggest interest. Your hottest leads are those who ask questions and interact a lot during the four-week online course. By following up with these people a few times you are more likely to make more sales.

WHY SOME MAKE NO SALES

When you go through the *Kickstart* process the first time you may not make any sales and there could be several reasons why:

• You had less than thirty-three signups for your free course. The average sales conversion in online business is three percent; three percent from thirty-two signups is less than one and therefore no sale is absolutely normal.

• You didn't have ideal clients in your free online course. Despite your intention of attracting only dream clients you widened the net and attracted non-ideal clients. You cannot sell to non-ideal clients.

• Your next online program wasn't the next natural step. Even though your participants told you clearly through feedback what they want you may have had different ideas of what you wanted to offer – and that doesn't sell.

The fact you didn't make sales the first time you went through *Kickstart* doesn't mean that you failed. It means that you need to go and tweak your ideal client or your offer or make sure you get more signups next time.

BEING GRATEFUL

Making sales at the end of the *Kickstart* process is the icing on the cake. In the original version of *Kickstart* (SOMBA Summer School) the plan was only to create an online course that you could sell again and again. At the very last minute I got the idea that my students could make an upsell. Everyone loved the idea, including those who didn't make any sales because at least they learned how to make an offer even if they didn't sell.

Without sales, it may feel as if the whole thing was a waste of time. Nothing could be further from the truth. That's why I want to remind you of the original goal of *Kickstart*. The *Kickstart* process is about meeting your ideal client, finding out what they want, designing a course that they want, promoting an online course to attract your dream clients, creating the online course with your ideal clients, so it becomes exactly what they want, getting feedback and testimonials, and finally celebrating together with your participants what you've all achieved. You've created an asset in your online business - a four-week online course - that you can sell again and again.

Building an online business takes time, and you need to be patient and nurture your ideal clients until they are ready to buy. After *Kickstart*, you have an email list full of future buyers. Take good care of them, and they will buy from you - even if they didn't buy instantly.

Svenja Hirsch is a non-fiction book writing coach and co-author for those who don't want to write themselves. She made only one sale during *Kickstart* and what some might think was a failure was actually the start of her online success. Even though the participants in her free four-week online course didn't buy right away, they started to buy later.

Svenja Hirsch's *Kickstart* experience in her own words:

"I had been a freelancer for a long time, then took a part time job which I lost. When I invested in *Kickstart* I was receiving unemployment benefits and had no regular income. Before *Kickstart* I had sold a couple of one-on-one book mentorings but it wasn't enough but I didn't know how to make more sales. I had only thirty people on my list and my confidence was very low.

With *Kickstart* I increased my self confidence and got rid of my overthinking. I rediscovered my passion and energy by following the steps, trusting the process and being supported by others who had similar problems to me.

After *Kickstart* I had around 130 people on my email list, one one-on-one client, lots of great testimonials - but the best for me was to know and FEEL how great I am in what I am doing. Because it worked so well in *Kickstart*.

One year later my email list is three times bigger and some of those people are from that first *Kickstart* round. They are now buying my programs because I took the time to nurture them and send them regular emails and offers."

Besides gratefulness, there are a couple of other mindset challenges you should be aware of in the *Kickstart* process that we will tackle in the next chapter.

12

OBSTACLES YOU MIGHT
ENCOUNTER

There are several obstacles on the way to creating your first or next online course and building a successful online business.

Most women I work with think that technology will be their biggest obstacle, and they are surprised to find out that the tech isn't actually that complicated. The usability of software tools has changed dramatically in the last decade. It used to be quite difficult to deliver an online course, but now the tools are so easy to use that anyone – literally anyone, even those who think of themselves as technically-challenged – can overcome all their tech challenges. In our *Kickstart* program, we have detailed instructions and step-by-step videos that show exactly how to do everything so that everyone who joins our program can master the technology needed for an online course.

The real obstacle is mindset.

You might have one or more thoughts like these:

- Someone else has already created a course on this, so why would anyone want to join my course?
- Who am I to offer an online course on this topic, I'm not an expert or a certified coach?
- I don't really want my family and friends to know what I am doing so I am not going to promote on my personal profiles.
- I don't want too many people to join my online course, I just want to keep it small so I can take good care of everyone.
- I just want to create an online course; do I really need to promote it so much?
- I am not going to make an offer on the celebration call, it feels too salesy to sell my free course participants something.

Let's tackle each of these mindset challenges one by one.

SOMEONE ELSE HAS ALREADY CREATED A COURSE ON THIS TOPIC

The fact that someone else out there has a course on the same or similar topic as you want to create, is excellent. That means that there is a market for your online course too. It is basically proof that your online course will sell. If that doesn't convince you, think of someone who wants to develop a new car. Should they not do that just because there are already so many car brands out there? That doesn't make any sense. There is always a market for new and different brands. Your online course is going to be different because it is created by you, and you are different, and that's why people will want to buy it from you.

WHO AM I TO OFFER AN ONLINE COURSE ON THIS TOPIC?

The imposter syndrome is real, and most women suffer from it. They don't see themselves as an expert on a topic even though they are, in other people's eyes, an absolute go-to-expert. They are worried that they will get questions that they cannot answer even though it is totally okay for experts – or anyone for that matter – to say, "I don't know," or "Let me check that for you."

Many worry to be "found out" or to phrase it differently; they are concerned that someone will one day realize that they aren't good enough. When you see someone else suffer from imposter syndrome you realize how ridiculous it is to have all these doubts. The best way to get rid of the imposter syndrome, is to face the fear and do it anyway. Slowly but surely, the imposter syndrome will be ridiculed out of your life.

I DON'T REALLY WANT MY FAMILY AND FRIENDS TO KNOW WHAT I AM DOING

If you want to build an online business, you need to be willing to use your personal profiles to promote whatever you are marketing and selling. I totally understand that it is hard in the beginning to expose yourself like that, but you'll get over it and the sooner you get over it the better. You cannot and should not hide from anyone what you are doing because any opportunity to talk about your business is a chance to attract more ideal clients and make more sales. This is of course easier when you are a part of a program like *Kickstart* where hundreds of other women are also overcoming this hurdle at the same time, and you feel supported to take this step.

I DON'T WANT TOO MANY PEOPLE TO JOIN MY ONLINE COURSE

The whole point of creating an online course is to be able to serve a lot of people at the same time. Instead of trading time for money, you are building an endlessly scalable online course that can serve ten, 100, or 1,000 people at the same time without you having to work more hours. Since you are offering a free four-week course when you run it for the first time, you want as many people as possible to participate. Not everyone who signs up will participate in your online course; therefore, you need more people, so you potentially have more that participate. After the course is finished, you are going to make an offer for the next step, and that's when it really matters to have a lot of people in your online course. That's why you shouldn't limit the number of participants in your free four-week course.

DO I REALLY NEED TO PROMOTE IT SO MUCH?

It's essential to promote your online course as much as you can. The first time you do this, it may feel like you are overdoing it. You may get worried about promoting too much. This feeling is normal and like with any other mindset challenges you encounter during this process, you will overcome it. You may also be concerned about being too salesy, but you aren't actually selling. Your first online course is free and therefore, it will not feel salesy when you promote it. You are doing your ideal client a favor by promoting your online course. You are being of service to offer your online course, and it is your job as someone who wants to help others to promote your course as much as possible – otherwise, people will not be able to receive your help.

I AM NOT GOING TO MAKE AN OFFER ON THE CELEBRATION CALLS

A business that doesn't make any sales is just an expensive hobby. You are not going through the *Kickstart* process to create an expensive hobby but to create a sustainable and profitable online business. Sales are the fuel of any business, and as a business owner (or future business owner), you need to get comfortable with selling. Think of selling as a service. You have a solution to a problem that someone has. They want to pay you for that solution. If you don't sell them the solution you have, then you are stealing. You are stealing away from them the joy of having their problem solved. You wouldn't want to steal from your ideal client, would you? Of course not, that's why you are going to make an offer, and you are going to have an opportunity to make sales.

It is normal to have obstacles when doing something new. It is part of our personal and professional growth to overcome obstacles. With every obstacle you overcome, you build your self-confidence, and then the next obstacle becomes easier. In fact, obstacles never go away; we just meet new obstacles that we need to overcome – that is how life and business works. I like to say that building your own business, especially an online business based on your personal brand, is the biggest personal development journey you'll ever go on.

WHAT'S NEXT FOR YOU

T housands have successfully gone through the *Kickstart* process in the last few years. And now, you can go through it too, either on your own by implementing what you've read, or with our support in the *Kickstart* program.

We run the *Kickstart* program live once or twice a year, and within ten weeks, over ninety percent of our students have created their first or next online course and had the opportunity to make money with their upsell. In only ten weeks, they go through the whole process that I've described in this book. It is a step-by-step process to help you create your first or next online course and start to make sales.

HOW TO SELL YOUR FOUR-WEEK ONLINE COURSE

The Kickstart process is about creating an online course that helps you make sales in your online business. It doesn't cover how to sell your four-week online course.

This may come as a surprise to you and that's why I will briefly cover how to sell your online course after you finish the *Kickstart* process. There are two main ways to sell a four-week online course, launching and evergreen.

• Launching

  ○ You can launch your online course which means you'll create a marketing campaign and sell your online course. If you would like to learn how to do this we have a program called Launch & Sell. Launching an online course is at least a 10-week process that includes planning the launch, designing a launch training, promoting the launch training, writing the sales page, writing invite emails, writing launch emails, writing sales emails, running the launch, selling during open cart, following up with those who show interest and so much more. In our Launch & Sell program we take you step by step through this whole process and give you all the templates you need so you can successfully launch your online course.

• Evergreen

  ○ You can evergreen your four-week online course which means people can buy it any time and you run it all the time. If you would like to learn how to do this we have a program called Sales Every Day. Evergreening an online course is at least a 10-week process that includes creating a freebie related to the online course, writing the copy for landing pages and sales pages, setting up the automation so that shows different price points depending on where people are in the automation, writing emails and automating delivery of the emails, setting up paid ads, optimizing the ads and the automation and so much more. In our Sales Every Day program we take you step by step through this whole process and give you all the templates you need so that you can start to have sales every day in your online business.

THE KICKSTART JOURNEY

Every *Kickstart* journey is different but what all our *Kickstart* graduates have in common is that *Kickstart* kick started their online business journey on the way to six and seven figures.

Frida Trönnberg helps women with pelvic floor pain through yoga. When the pandemic hit she had to quickly take her offline business online. Within four months of joining *Kickstart* Frida was making six figures in her online business.

Frida Trönnberg's *Kickstart* experience in her own words:

"I teach yoga for pain relief to women who have pelvic problems. Having suffered from a severe birth injury myself, I didn't get any help from the health care system at the time. I educated and learned how to heal myself, and started offering workshops and classes with exercises in different cities in Sweden.

Then COVID-19 hit, and I had to switch from offline to online classes. I knew that the situation wouldn't change anytime soon, and I started to see the benefits of fully taking my business online. It's important that women who take part in my classes feel safe and have privacy, and attending from their own homes instead of a studio full of other people was giving them just that.

Also, it became clear to me that I was able to scale and reach more people, and by developing courses, I would finally have more time to spend with my family. I had another job as a political scientist, so having more time was very precious to me.

A friend of mine was in one of Sigrun's programs, and since she's very successful with her online business, I asked her whether it would be something that could help me, too. However, I was so busy at the time that I never took part in any of Sigrun's free webinars or classes. When I received the very last reminder to sign up for SOMBA, I decided to go for it.

I participated in *Kickstart*, the ten-week sprint in which I was going to create an online course. When I received 1350 sign ups, I knew I was on to something. It was such a big number, and I realized that what I had was a good business idea.

What I loved about *Kickstart* was that I could just trust the process. Receiving all the material at once would have been overwhelming, so I really appreciated the week-by-week structure. I never had to think of the next step - I just followed the process. There was also not much philosophical talk about creating an online business - we could have spent years figuring that out - the focus was on taking action instead of making everything perfect. The support from the group and mentors was extremely valuable and I've made friends for life!

At the end, I presented my offer: A ten-week online course for $745. At first, sales started to drip in very slowly and doubts formed in my head. But as the deadline of my open cart approached, more and more women signed up. I ended up making $31,000 in my first launch!

In November I launched my program again, this time as a six-week online course for $407. I made 75 sales resulting in $31,000 a second time, and then I added a downsell. The final result of my launch was $35,000.

My third launch shortly afterward also resulted in over $30,000. Four months after going online, I was running a six-figure online business!

Six months after joining *Kickstart* I quit my job as a political scientist and focused solely on helping women heal from pelvic pain with my online business."

Like so many of our *Kickstart* students, Nicola Lederer had created an online course that didn't sell so well. So she joined *Kickstart* to create an online course that would sell. A year after she joined Kickstart Nicole had reached six figures in her online business.

Nicola Lederer's *Kickstart* experience in her own words:

"I quit my job as head of marketing in 2017 to follow my passion: photography. I started offering photography courses in Vienna, Austria. Very soon I realized that I wanted to create an online course, which I did in 2019. I worked weeks on that course and when it was finished, I tried to sell it. But no one bought it. I lowered the price and had a couple of sales. But it was not enough to make a living.

It was January 2020 when I tried to launch the course another time. It was better than before, but still - not enough to make a living. I sold six spots for €249. And I was so afraid to go for this price, I thought it was way too expensive.

Then I heard of Sigrun. I signed up for her free workshop and was impressed by how much information she was giving away. And then there was her offer. I knew this could be the right thing for me. But investing so much money when there was zero income? Back then I did not have the mindset that one has to invest in order to gain.

I talked to friends and family and everyone said: go for it. So I signed up. And then I learned about the different formats I could sell and for the first time I sold one-on-one photography coaching for €997. I sold three spots and had my investment back within the ten weeks of *Kickstart*. After another ten weeks I launched my group coaching program and had my first 5-figure launch. I continued to launch, refined the group coaching program, and in 2021 I reached my first six-figure year."

Our students talk about before and after *Kickstart*, like Lucie Samková. Before *Kickstart* she didn't know anything about online business and after *Kickstart* Lucie had a thriving online business helping teachers with formative assessments.

Lucie Samková's *Kickstart* experience in her own words:

"I was thinking about joining *Kickstart* for a very long time. Then I decided and joined *Kickstart* in January 2021. I got money from my husband to pay for it... After *Kickstart* I had all the money I invested back and so much more... After *Kickstart* I had almost 3000 people on my email list and two online courses...

Kickstart really changed my life and business."

Kickstart doesn't just help you kick start your online business, it also increases your self-confidence and many of our students report that they feel happier like Brigita Ložar.

Brigita Ložar's *Kickstart* experience in her own words:

"I am a mom of two kids (now ages seven and four) and a wife to a wonderful husband, who works as a mayor in our small town. I have always been creative with my hands and loved acting and singing. I worked in a court of law as a typist for about 15 years. In the middle of the Covid-19 crisis, when the world practically stopped, I had time to talk to myself about what I really want and where I really want to be. This is when I realized, I don't want to have a 9 to 5 job that does not fulfill me anymore.

It was when I finished the five-day workshop with Sigrun and enrolled in *Kickstart*, I finally decided to take action. Quitting my formal job and starting as an entrepreneur with online sewing courses was the best thing happening to me in a long time. I started enjoying life more, loving what I do for a living and consequently, I am a happier and healthier person now."

Some of our students say they were lost before *Kickstart* and now they've found their purpose and meaning in life like Blanca Vergara.

Blanca Vergara's *Kickstart* experience in her own words:

"Before *Kickstart* my life was a hot mess. In less than one week I buried three family members, among them my mother. Grieving while caring for my family pushed my business to the background. I had set up a coaching practice ten years before. This practice was always small, growing by word of mouth with little to no online presence. My income was tiny, just enough to pay for some fun for the family. I was constantly doubting myself, moving in one direction, and as I got impatient I moved in

another direction. My brand and messaging were incon-
sistent, so was my income and my personal satisfaction..

The most important change was that I found my voice
and my people. Every day I'm becoming more and more
centered in my purpose. Every day I'm becoming more
and more self-expressed in my business. And that
wouldn't have happened without *Kickstart*."

Kickstart is the fast-track to your online business
success, according to Deimante Prismantaite. It helps you
achieve more in ten weeks than you would in five years.

Deimante Prismantaite's *Kickstart* experience in her own
words:

"The best thing about *Kickstart* is that it helps you create
an online course, and it shows you how to do it professionally. There are step-by-step instructions for everything, you only have to decide yourself what it is you are
going to teach. There is no time for procrastination, overthinking, doubting, none of that. But there is enough time
to take action. And in ten weeks you learn more than you
could learn in perhaps five years by yourself."

Kickstart is in another league according to Kerstin
Sönnichen.

Kerstin Sönnichen's *Kickstart* experience in her own
words:

"What I like about *Kickstart* is that it is super compact and
really a fast-track. It is tough and you might start sweating
and/or have short nights during those ten weeks. And you
might think at more than one point that you might not

make it. But when you cope with the pace you will earn a lot. And in the overall marathon of an online business, *Kickstart* is the fast-track to more success in a separate row. I don't know any other program which forces and empowers you to bring you forward in the way *Kickstart* does."

Kickstart is for action takers according to Jana Hájková.

Jana Hájková's *Kickstart* experience in her own words:

"I started my online business in January 2020 but until I joined *Kickstart* in Summer 2021 I just kept myself busy (as you often and truthfully say). :-)

Before *Kickstart* I was sort of studying and educating myself in various aspects of online business but didn't take much action. In my heart, I am an action taker and everything I experienced in *Kickstart* was the right way of working for me.

I loved being told what to focus on each week and very much valued the sessions with the coaches and the mentors. I was also amazed how valuable the breakout-rooms were. Speaking to other entrepreneurs going through the same process was so helpful.

Kickstart was my best business decision ever!"

INVITATION TO JOIN OUR KICKSTART PROGRAM

Now you've read this book and it is time to take action. You are welcome to follow the steps laid out in this book to create your own *Kickstart* success, create your first or next online course, and start to make sales online.

By joining our next round of *Kickstart* your success is

literally guaranteed. In our program, the *Kickstart* process is explained in a lot more detail than is possible in this book, and includes step-by-step videos that show you exactly what to do, how to do it, and when to do it including all the technical setup you need to achieve your goals. Our support is unprecedented, we have coaches and mentors who are there to help you whenever you need any help. Our motto is "no one left behind" when it comes to support. In addition to weekly coaching calls, breakout sessions, and coaching in our community, we also have an unbeatable accountability system that ensures that everyone stays on track and finishes on time. This is how we can achieve a ninety percent completion rate and can confidently say that your success is literally guaranteed by joining our program.

I'm inviting you to join the *Kickstart* Insider List so you'll be notified the next time doors open to the program – plus you'll be able to secure some Insider Bonuses. Go to www.sigrun.com/kickstartbook to sign up and get access to all our free *Kickstart* resources.

ACKNOWLEDGMENTS

This is my very first book and my first book in a series to help women fast-track their seven-figure online success. In this book, I talk about many of the obstacles that women face when they are building their online businesses. I faced my own obstacles in writing this book. It was like the Universe was testing me, seeing how badly I wanted to write this book.

The first obstacle was a two-month family emergency just around the time where I was supposed to hand in the first draft of my book. This family emergency had a bigger impact on me than I cared to admit. I completely lost my energy, so even after the family emergency was over and everyone was safe and sound at home, I didn't have the energy to focus on writing. Once I started to gain some of my energy again the next obstacle appeared.

The second obstacle was an accident where I hurt both my wrists just around the time where I was supposed to hand in the final manuscript of my book. I was wearing new sneakers and it was raining outside when I slipped on a manhole cover. I felt excruciating pain and realized something really bad had happened. I broke my left wrist and sprained the right one so I couldn't use both arms for a while. Luckily the right one healed in two weeks but the left one was in cast for six and a half weeks and was still not fully healed when I wrote the last chapter of this book.

My third obstacle was getting Covid-19 just when I had handed in my final manuscript and wanted to work on my book cover. Despite having asthma since I was twelve years old and weak lungs after a virus infection a year earlier, I got a mild case of Covid with only one really bad day. After ten days I had almost fully recovered and could continue my book project.

My fourth obstacle was my mindset. I kept postponing writing this book even though I knew exactly what I was going to write. It was like I wanted to sabotage my own success. The lizard brain (the negative voice in your head) was having a field day when it succeeded in me postponing my writing one more time. But just like I help others start and scale their online businesses to seven figures with coaching and accountability, I had the accountability and support I needed to finish this book and the lizard brain didn't have a chance.

I want to thank Angela Lauria and her team at Author Incubator for their unwavering support and understanding but also their excellent accountability and tough love to help me write and finish this book despite all the obstacles I faced. Special thanks to my editor Madeline Kosten who was with me all the way to the finish line.

I want to thank my husband, Martin Uetz, for his encouragement and endless support when it comes to following my dreams. He is my biggest supporter and at the same time my toughest critic and understands what it takes to achieve success.

I want to thank my parents, Guðjón Jónsson and Ásta Bjarnadóttir, for being the best parents I could have asked for. I thank them for instilling in me the belief that I can do anything. Also thanks to them I believe in love.

I want to thank my team at Sigrun GmbH who have stood by my side and helped me run the company through all the challenges that I've faced while writing this book. When my energy was the lowest we managed to have a 7-

figure launch against all odds. Special thanks goes to Laura Phillips for stepping in as our launch manager last-minute. Slowly I found my energy back with my team's support.

I want to especially thank Natalie Christy Janine Hewett, our Chief Operating Officer, and Natasha Vorompiova, for their extraordinary support - and for reviewing the final manuscript, not just once but twice. I couldn't have done this without the two of you.

I also want to give our *Kickstart* Headcoach Rosalie Audoin a shout out for making sure we continue to achieve a ninety percent completion rate in our *Kickstart* program. In addition, I want to thank the rest of Team Sigrun for keeping our other programs running flawlessly. Thank you Merilyn Beretta, Hannah Mang, Kat Bern and Sif Traustadóttir. You are the best team ever!

There are many former team members who have also helped make Kickstart what it is today. I want to thank Anke Beeren for being our first *Kickstart* coach and helping me shape the program so that it can be easily run again and again. I want to thank Lynn Rivest, our former marketing director, for helping me market and launch this amazing program.

Without all the mentors that have supported us in *Kickstart*, I would never have been able to go into the second round of SOMBA Summer School and continue to provide high quality support and unprecedented accountability. I want to thank all the wonderful mentors who have ensured that all our students get all the help they need. Our mentors are current or former students who have gone through the *Kickstart* process themselves and now want to help our students have an amazing *Kickstart* experience. The first time I worked with mentors was in SOMBA Summer School 2019. Twenty students volunteered to help me run the program. I was blown away by the support in the community. After that summer, being a mentor became a paid part-time role, and we have always had numerous mentors during every round of *Kickstart*. I want to thank all our amazing mentors since 2019 and especially those who have been supporting us already for several quarters like Ina Mewis, Luisa Tuzza, Kerstin Sönnichsen, Svenja Hirsch, and Rachael Watt.

Special thanks to my sister, Gyða Guðjónsdóttir, for proofreading the manuscript, not just once but three times, and giving me excellent feedback that has helped me make this book even easier to read and understand. I feel so lucky to have you as my sister.

Last but not least, I want to thank Lisa Larter for writing the foreword to this book. Few years ago, I was the one reviewing and proofreading her first book before it was published. Back then I thought to myself, one day I want to write a book like hers. You are holding this book in your hands now.

ABOUT THE AUTHOR

Sigrun is on a mission to accelerate gender equality through female entrepreneurship. She is an award-winning business coach, international speaker, and host of a top-rated podcast. Originally from Reykjavik, Iceland, she has spent half her life outside her home country, in Germany, United Kingdom, and Switzerland.

Sigrun was always drawn to leadership roles, so despite having zero business background nor the education, she made a life-changing phone call and asked to become the CEO of a software company in Iceland shortly after finishing her master's degree in architecture – and she got the job!

Ten years, another three master's degrees, and several CEO roles later, Sigrun found herself in Switzerland with her newfound love but sick and unemployable. Her dream was to be location independent so she could split her time between Iceland and Switzerland, travel the world, and take care of her health.

So, in 2014, Sigrun started her online business and quickly built a multiple seven figure coaching business. Now she's made over $10M in revenue and helped over 5000 women from all over the world start and scale their online businesses to six and seven figures with her tough love and no-nonsense-approach to business and life.

Kickstart Your Online Business is her first book and the first book in the Fast-Track to 7 Figures series.

ABOUT DIFFERENCE PRESS

Difference Press is the publishing arm of The Author Incubator, an Inc. 500 award-winning company that helps business owners and executives grow their brand, establish thought leadership, and get customers, clients, and highly-paid speaking opportunities, through writing and publishing books.

While traditional publishers require that you already have a large following to guarantee they make money from sales to your existing list, our approach is focused on using a book to grow your following -- even if you currently don't have a following. This is why we charge an up-front fee but never take a percentage of revenue you earn from your book.

☞ MORE THAN A COACH. MORE THAN A PUBLISHER. ✍

We work intimately and personally with each of our authors to develop a revenue-generating strategy for the book. By using a Lean Start Up style methodology, we guarantee the book's success before we even start writing. We provide all the technical support authors need with editing, design, marketing, and publishing, the emotional support you would get from a book coach to help you manage anxiety and time constraints, and we serve as a strategic thought partner engineering the book for success.

The Author Incubator has helped almost 2,000 entrepreneurs write, publish, and promote their non-fiction books. Our authors have used their books to gain international media exposure, build a brand and marketing following, get highly-paid speaking engagements, raise awareness of their product or service, and attract clients and customers.

☞ ARE YOU READY TO WRITE A BOOK? ✍

As a client, we will work with you to make sure your book gets done right and that it gets done quickly. The Author Incubator provides one-stop for strategic book consultation, author coaching to manage writer's block and anxiety, full-service professional editing, design, and self-publishing services, and book marketing and launch campaigns. We sell this as one package so our clients are not slowed down with contradictory advice. We have a 99% success rate with nearly all of our clients completing their books, publishing them, and reaching bestseller status upon launch.

☞ APPLY NOW AND BE OUR NEXT SUCCESS STORY ✍

To find out if there is a significant ROI for you to write a book, get on our calendar by completing an application at www.TheAuthorIncubator.com/apply.

OTHER BOOKS BY DIFFERENCE PRESS

The Scholarship Playbook for Parents of Student-Athletes: Stop Fouling Out and Start Scoring Money for College by Dr. Simoné Edwards

Longevity: Reinvent Yourself at Any Age by Maria L. Ellis, MBA

Leadership Parenting: Empower Your Child's Social Success by Mother Gopi Gita

Embracing Equity: Best Practices for Developing and Keeping a Winning Multi-Racial Leadership Team by Janine Hill, PhD

Weight Loss for High Achievers: Stop Self-Sabotage and Start Losing Weight by Karen King

When Marriage Needs a Miracle: The Modern Woman's Guide to Figure out the Future of Your Relationship by Shari Kubinec

The Speed of Passion: How Relationship-Based Leadership Drives Innovation by Carol Ann Langford

Profitable Online Programs: A Brief Guide to Creating and Launching an Impactful Digital Course, Then Scaling Your Biz with Your Own Expert Book! by Dr. Angela E. Lauria

Take Back Your Life: Find Hope and Freedom from Fibromyalgia Symptoms and Pain by Tami Stackelhouse

The $7-Trillion Shock Wave: 401K Investing Strategies with a Positive Impact in Our Shared Climate Future by Seann Stoner

Understanding the Profiles in Human Design: The Facilitator's Guide to Unleashing Potential by Robin Winn, MFT

THANK YOU

Thank you so much for reading *Kickstart Your Online Business: Create An Online Course and Start to Make Sales.* Since you've made it this far I know a couple of things about you. First, you are a reader just like me. Second, you want to kick off your online business. Third, maybe you just got here before you read the book?! No cheating, go back to the beginning ;-)

Wondering how to really get started and kick start your online business? Find out how you can get started today by claiming your free gifts at www.sigrun.com/kickstartbook.

Creating an online course, building your email list, and making your first sales online - is just the beginning of building your online business. Next you want to continue growing your email list and start to make sales every day with automation (evergreen). Then you want to learn how to launch and sell your online course and ultimately you want to also create and sell high-end scalable programs. My team and I have programs for female online entrepreneurs who are just starting out and also those who are making five, six, or even seven figures in their online business. You can find out more at www.sigrun.com.

Online business is one of the best ways for women to start their own business. It requires a low investment to get started and enables women to work from home if they want to. When more women start and scale their online businesses, more women will become financially independent, and are able to provide for their families. When women make more money, they have more opportunities. More opportunities create more equality.

I'm on a mission to accelerate gender equality through female entrepreneurship and online business is my way to inspire and empower women to make their dreams come true. Together we can make the world a better place.

I want to leave you with this quote from my role model, former president of Iceland, Vigdís Finnbogadóttir: "I think, if the world can be saved, it will be by women."

Printed in Great Britain
by Amazon

39954037R00086